BUDDHISM AND THE NATURAL WORLD

P. D. RYAN

BUDDHISM AND
THE NATURAL WORLD

Towards a Meaningful Myth

WINDHORSE PUBLICATIONS

Published by Windhorse Publications
11 Park Road
Birmingham
B13 8AB

Cover design Dhammarati
Pāli consultant Katherine Keller
Printed by Interprint Ltd, Marsa, Malta
Cover image Steven Edson/Photonica

British Library Cataloguing in Publication Data:
A catalogue record for this book is available from the British Library

ISBN   1 899579 00 1

The publishers wish to acknowledge with gratitude permission to quote extracts
from the following:

p.32 & p.64. We quote by permission of Gower Publishing Ltd., Aldershot, which
owns the copyright in Trevor Ling, *The Buddha*, Penguin, Harmondsworth 1976
p.55 & p.77. Edward J. Thomas, *The Life of Buddha as Legend and History*,
Routledge & Kegan Paul, London 1975, pp.32–33 and p.207
p.61. We quote by permission of Beacon Press which owns the copyright in Max
Scheler, *Man's Place in Nature*, trans. Hans Meyerhoff, Farrar Straus and Giroux,
New York 1981
p.74. ed. George A. Panichas, *Irving Babbitt: Representative Writings*, University of
Nebraska, Lincoln, Nebraska 1981

We quote by permission of the Pali Text Society which owns the copyright in the
following works:

p.27 & p.37. T.W. & C.A.F. Rhys Davids (trans.), *Dialogues of the Buddha*,
part III, published by Luzac for the Pali Text Society, London 1971
pp.58–60. T.W. Rhys Davids (trans.), *Dialogues of the Buddha*, part I, London 1973

Every effort has been made to trace the copyright in the following. If any
omissions have been made please let us know so that this may be rectified in a
future edition.

p.49. David Maurice, *The Lion's Roar*
p.78. Edward Conze, *Buddhism: Its Essence and Development*

CONTENTS

About the Author

P. D. Ryan was born in Ireland. From an early age he was drawn to a view of life that he later found to be Buddhist. As a young man, he travelled extensively and worked in a variety of jobs, but a severe illness later in life prompted him to look at the world with a new seriousness. After his recovery he went back to formal education, taking a degree in Religious Studies, which included Linguistics and Indian Civilization.

It was while doing postgraduate studies that the ideas contained in this book came to him. In the Buddhist texts he found a radical doctrine which challenged many of his previous assumptions. The traditional teachings of the Buddha seemed to offer the answer to the social, moral, and environmental crises of our time.

References and Pronunciation

REFERENCES

Most of the texts used in this study are from the *Dīgha-* and *Majjhima-Nikāyas*; these titles are indicated by their initial letters, DN and MN, with Roman numerals used for the suttas. AN and SN stand for the *Aṅguttara-* and *Saṃyutta-Nikāyas* respectively.

The translation of the *Dīgha-Nikāya* by T.W. and C.A.F. Rhys Davids, entitled *Dialogues of the Buddha*, is indicated by the letters DB. Where not otherwise attributed, translations and paraphrases are by the author.

PRONUNCIATION OF PĀLI

a like 'u' in 'but'; ā like 'a' in 'par'; e long like the vowel sound in 'care', or short before a double consonant, as in 'bell'; i like 'i' in 'sit'; ī like 'i' in 'machine'; o long as in 'lo', or short before a double consonant, as in 'odd'; u like 'u' in 'put'; ū like 'u' in 'flu'.

Consonants are pronounced more or less as in English, but 'c' is always as in the Italian 'ciao'. Combined with 'h' to make a digraph (ch) it is sounded more breathily. Likewise the other digraphs, bh, dh, gh, jh, kh, ph, th, are pronounced more breathily than the unaccompanied b, d, etc. The palatal ñ is pronounced as in Spanish. Letters with an underdot (ḍ, ḍh, etc.) are sounded much as the undotted letters, but ṁ has a nasal quality.

To my wife, Bernice

INTRODUCTION

THESE PAGES ARE the record of a quest in Buddhist literature. The quest had a twofold purpose: to find out what the early Buddhists thought and felt about the natural world, and to see if that might have a meaning for our troubled time.

Anxieties over man's relations with the world are today universal, and a challenge no less to religious than to economic and political systems. The concerned layman may well ask why it is a sin to covet your neighbour's wife or property while it is no sin to wipe out the last few tiger, oryx, or gorilla in the world. From this it is but a short step to larger questions. What is the value of non-human life in the view of the various religions? What do the scriptures say their founders thought and felt about the world? These are not questions to be attempted lightly, but soon or late they will have to be answered, since religion bears a great, perhaps even the greatest, responsibility for man's dealings with the world. Most thinking people recognize that something is amiss, but we are not sure what it may be. We look through all the fields of intellect. The vistas are a blaze of brilliance but they give no ease. We are dazzled with knowledge while groping for wisdom.

That wisdom is to be found in the long course of history perhaps only a few, even at this disillusioned time, seriously doubt. But the wisdom of the Western tradition is inseparably bound up with the attitudes which have made the world what it is today. The hard dominantism of Genesis may yield to the idea of stewardship, but stewardship too is based on dominance and is open to all manner of abuse. Religions

outside the Judaic tradition have other attitudes and values. The fundamental postulate of Buddhism is that all living beings are united in
distress, in *dukkha*. In the truly atmospheric distress which is the element of reflective life today, it is reasonable to look beyond our received
cultural tradition. It may be too much to say that the world groans and
is in travail for the faults of this tradition, but it is one which has been
in love as much with power as with holiness. Today we see power going
its own way and no one knows how its progress will end. The value of
Buddhism is not least that from the first it has distrusted power. If I
may bring together two famous phrases of the modern era and give
them a Buddhist turn, to the assertion made at the beginning of the
scientific period that knowledge is power, it would reply that power
always corrupts. The first chapter of this book implicitly asks whether
the knowledge which gives rise to power may not also be corruptive.
Buddhism, based as it is on insight into human nature, cannot be other
than sceptical about the claims of any approach to reality described as
neutral, value-free, dispassionate among other gratulatory adjectives.
It does not accept that an ideal or a discipline or a method can be
considered apart from the human beings who devote themselves to it;
and as these are subject to passions and vices, so the knowledge they
cultivate will be, and will inexorably enlarge the operation of those
failings in the world. It says that detachment and dispassion are qualities no more natural to the man or woman of intellect than to anyone
else, nor conferred on them in virtue of their vocation. They are the
fruits of a moral rather than an intellectual culture and an individual
or a society that ignores this must soon or late come to grief. The three
'evil roots' of human nature in the Buddhist view are self-interest, ill-
will, and delusion (*rāga, dosa, moha*). The first duty of anyone aspiring
to detachment is to inquire how he stands in the light of this view, with
its affirmation that out of evil roots come evil fruits in the fullness of
time. Evil may be prodigal of gifts and benefits and we may call it good,
judging by these. But our self-deceptions cannot change its nature,
which is ultimately destructive, whatever the splendour of its inter-
mediate achievements. In honesty today we are bound to interrogate
not only what is self-evidently evil but much of what we have hitherto
accepted as good.

One of the great concerns of Buddhism is how we should relate to the
world around us, and yet, in English at least, the relevant texts seem

largely to have eluded study. There has been an ever-increasing literature on just about every aspect of Buddhism, from the subtleties of the
anattā doctrine to the humour of Zen, but rather less on the great
question of man's relations with the world and nature. It is as if the
staring magnitude of the problem had been lost to sight, or as if the
supposed unworldliness of Buddhism removed the need to deal with
it.

Fortunately there is now increasing evidence that this attitude is
changing, though perhaps mainly in respect of social and economic
aspects of the early Buddhist period. The question of relations with the
non-human world has received rather less consideration, especially in
the modern literature on the Theravadin tradition. Mahāyāna Buddhism has been better served, largely because of the Western fascination
with Zen, but even there it is often implied that it was Taoism which
brought the Mahāyāna down to earth and gave actuality to an aloof
and fastidious creed. But all Buddhist traditions trace their lines of
succession back to the same source, whatever other traditions may
have influenced them in their descent, and the early literature is the
nearest we can get to the thinking and attitudes of the Buddha and his
contemporaries. I hope to show that this literature demonstrates that
early Buddhism was a movement sympathetic and sensitive to the
natural world and indeed gave substance to the best aspirations of the
time in which the Wheel of the Law was set in motion.

Buddhist chronology has been worked out with a high though not
incontestable degree of accuracy. The earliest surviving form of the
doctrine in its entirety is the Canon of the Theravāda school written in
the Pāli language.* These texts are divided into three divisions called
Piṭakas, from a word meaning basket, and contain severally the discourses and dialogues of the Buddha (*Suttas*), the monastic discipline
(*Vinaya*), and the later scholastic writings (*Abhidhamma*). The Sutta

---

* It has to be remembered that the Dhamma was delivered orally and not in writing by
the Buddha, and transmitted orally by several generations of his followers. This largely
accounts for the repetitiveness of the texts, repetition being the great aid of memorizing.
The transmission was not uniform, however, and within a few hundred years of the
Buddha's death (around 480BC) there were some eighteen versions of the doctrine and
as many sects. Only the Pāli version survived entire. The Sanskrit versions, called not
nikāyas but āgamas, were subsequently translated into Chinese. The considerable
surviving portions enable us to know in some measure what united and what divided
the Buddhist community before the rise of the Mahāyāna. For further discussion of this
important matter, see Kenneth K.S. Ch'en, *Buddhism in China*, ch.xiii.

Piṭaka, the oldest part of the Canon, commands the widest authority. The Vinaya applies specifically to monks and nuns, and not to the vast majority of the Buddhist community. The Abhidhamma is a collection of scholastic treatises elaborated several centuries after the Buddha's death. They attempt to systematize the teachings found in the suttas. Although greatly admired by some authorities – Edward Conze describes its creation as 'one of the greatest achievements of the human intellect'* – the Abhidhamma has not been accepted by all the schools of Buddhism. Even in early times there were some which refused to accept it as canonical.

I have not drawn on the Abhidhamma in this book principally because it adds nothing to the Buddha's Teaching as found in the suttas, but also because its intensely analytical attitude may well have contributed to the general disregard of the Canon's mythical content. Analysis and imagination do not travel easily together.

The Sutta Piṭaka, on which this study is based, is itself divided into five divisions. In the first two, the *Dīgha-Nikāya* and the *Majjhima-Nikāya*, the doctrine is presented in the form of discourses and dialogues. In the third, the material is analysed and rearranged by subject, and in the fourth by number, that is, according as things can be listed in ones, twos, threes, and so on. The fifth division is vast and miscellaneous, containing among much else the very early verses of the Sutta Nipāta and the popular Birth Stories of the Buddha, the Jātaka tales, which are almost a literature in themselves. One of their most striking features is that the Buddha in former lives is sometimes depicted as an animal. To the early Buddhist community this was clearly a most natural thing.

'Myth' is one of the most emotive terms in religion. There are the ultra-rationalists to whom it is still the last word of dismissal: religion is nothing but myth, they say, and mean that religion is nothing. On the other hand, there are those who will not allow the least association of it with what they consider to be true religion, and see in the Book of Genesis virtually a scientific document. But science, too, has its myths, and its hold on the modern mind is much the same hold that myth has always had, since it derives its power from belief and from an almost unconscious acquiescence in its ability to make the only or at any rate the best sense of things. Between these extremes the middle ground has

* *A Short History of Buddhism*, p.55.

been all but lost, the fruitful ground where a religious understanding of myth may be cultivated. Yet there is hardly to be found a mythic theme which does not deal with concerns close to the heart of religion. Indeed, it might not be too bold to go a step further and say that myth is the heart of religion and that when religion looks at myth it looks into its own secret being.

The greatest myths are the creation stories. These are much more than patches of anthropology on the walls of the past. They represent the first and arguably the greatest step in the intellectual history of the human race and its various peoples. A creation story is the fruit of the first wide awakening of mind to the mystery of the world's presence. It is an answer to the first transcendental question, as stories of a fall are answers to the first subjective question. That our ancestors gave such various and fascinating answers is less significant than the fact that the questions occurred to them at all, and that they had a mind equal to the now near inconceivable tremendousness of the task. What with the uncertainty of his future, his precarious present, and the perplexity of the remembered past, it is the most astonishing thing that man should have turned his thoughts further and further back, that he should have conceived of a time older than memory, and that he had the strength of mind to enter and to work in that darkness. Out of the darkness he emerged with light and set afoot the long hermeneutics of myth, history, science, and religion, trying to make sense of the mysteries pressing in upon him every night and day. It was a task of imagination and intellect together. Later ages are not called on to do anything so extraordinary. But myths have to be reinterpreted, just as religion has to be reformed, science rethought, and history written from previously unconsidered viewpoints. Sometimes a myth is so overshadowed by other elements in the tradition that it has virtually to be rediscovered. This study is in part about such a quest.

The Buddha as mythopoeist is not a familiar figure in the history of religions, nor is his story of the origins of the world and society a familiar myth. Coomaraswamy's *Myths of the Hindus and Buddhists*, with no shortage of kalpas and yugas and other cosmological arithmetic, has no mention of it. Closer to our own time, Eliade in his very comprehensive anthology of myth and religion, *From Primitives to Zen*, is also unaware of it. He has a number of selections from Buddhist literature, including the Pāli Canon, but nothing, among all the myths of origin, about the *Aggañña Sutta* (DN.xxvi), the myth attributed to the

Buddha himself. Other writers and anthologists fail just as surprisingly to take notice of it. But then, Buddhists themselves have paid it much less attention than it merits, perhaps because of the strong rationalistic tendency of the Buddhist revival in Asia. It is understandable that this should be so, and indeed that people may be uncomfortable with something which by definition is not respectably rational. But the *Aggañña Sutta* is, as I hope to show, among other things a potent statement of Buddhist values, a fascinating synthesis of cosmology and ethics.

A curious feature of modern thought is the equation of anonymity and unconsciousness. It is assumed that myths, legends, and fairy-tales are productions of the unconscious, largely on the ground that no personal authorship is attached to them. The assumption may reflect the gross individualism of our age more than its psychological wisdom. What is impersonal is seen as falling short of full identity. On the past we turn the eyes of bureaucrats: no name, no existence. We do not apply this standard in all cases; visible, physical facts mitigate our certainties. A cave painting, a medieval cathedral, even the crudest fetish: we do not insist that these came out of the unconscious without some singular, personal activity. Neither do we insist that a folk melody is the unconscious bursting into song. But when we move into the verbal-intellectual sphere all manner of licence seems to be allowable. Not that myth is commonly regarded as pertaining to the intellectual sphere in its own right; that only comes to be when we have theorized it. And theorizing involves a devaluation. Not only do we say that the myth proceeds from the unconscious, we say that it represents the unconscious; by which token we set ourselves up as representing the conscious – the rational, the enlightened – both in respect of the mind and in respect of history. We proclaim ourselves wiser than the past: we – unconsciously – tout the myth of progress. If the past was wise, it was so unknowingly; it was wise without being truly conscious, and was thus not truly wise. We shed our light back on the past. A dark, blind wisdom glimmers to us in a profundity unguessed by its first possessors. The ancients had no idea what treasures lay in their old stories; they were, it would seem, rather like fish swimming in 'the dark unfathomed caves of ocean', unconscious of the 'gems of purest ray serene' around them. Not the least interesting feature of the Buddhist creation story is that it is given as a perfectly conscious myth, attributed to the Buddha on a specific occasion in answer to a specific problem. For all we know, the same may hold good of other great myths except that the names of their originators have been lost. We do not have to subscribe to the theory of the unconscious to account for them.

My reading of the *Aggañña Sutta* has led me to the belief that it comprehends the meaning of Buddhism in a more potent form than much ordinary doctrinal exposition; and that anyone who has accepted Buddhism will get a stronger sense of what our relations with nature ought to be if he penetrates to the message of its myth. Some authorities see in the discourse primarily a satire on Vedic mythology. The two young men to whom it is delivered are brahmans, which means that Vedic myth, hymn, and ritual have shaped their lives. Central to this system was the belief that the brahmans were the highest of the four castes, an idea contrary to the Buddhist belief that deeds meant more than birth. A good deal of Buddhist criticism was directed at the pretensions of the brahmans and indeed at the hollowness of their ideas of the gods. Some of it is humorous and, interestingly, the humour has worn well, through two and a half millennia. Certainly in the *Aggañña Sutta* there is satire, but there is much more besides.

Others see the discourse as a parable. Like the stories in the Gospel, it points a moral. But there the comparison ends. The Gospel stories are like short narrative poems; the *Aggañña Sutta* has the movement of an epic. Like all exemplary stories it is open to many interpretations. A recent translator interestingly interprets it in the light of the Vinaya, the monastic Code of Discipline.* But one can view it very differently. I think it refers to something more universal. Its cosmic sweep and vital treatment of ideas raise it to the level of myth. My hope is to show that it is for our time a meaningful myth.

But before this can be realized, a good deal of preparatory work needs to be done. The early chapters of this book are an attempt at least to indicate what some of this work may be.

The first problem is the transcultural one of terminology. Occasionally when reading about other times and other societies, one has the uneasy feeling that different human groups may inhabit quite different worlds from that of one's own experience – the world until that point taken for granted, the experience until then unthinkingly universalized. The differences may be gross or they may be subtle, yet remain

---

* Steven Collins, 'The Discourse on What is Primary (Aggañña Sutta)'.

all unnoticed until one tries to come to terms with the language in which an alien culture expresses itself. To us, for instance, the word 'nature' means a great deal, though if pressed we may not be immediately able to say precisely what; but it is something more or less definite; and we know or guess that other peoples using other forms of the Latin word *natura* mean something more or less the same. They have similar viewpoints and values, being heirs of a common civilization, broadly speaking. However, when we leave Europe behind and converse with alien cultures this in varying degrees no longer holds. With Buddhist literature there is less sense of alienness than sometimes with religions better known in the West; although so distant in time, the problems which the Buddha was called upon to face are often strangely contemporary with our problems today. When difficulties are encountered they may sometimes be traced to disaccord between key terms in the languages. Some crucial Pāli terms have no satisfactory equivalents in English or in the major European languages, while some words which we take most for granted assume a problematical aspect in the light of a Pāli dictionary. 'Nature' is one of them.

The Canon has a number of terms corresponding in a general way with various aspects of what the word signifies; also a number transcending its scope as generally accepted in the West; but there is none which in all its applications may be rendered by the word 'nature' alone. These Pāli terms are important in the exposition of Buddhist doctrine. In addition they convey a sense of how the early Buddhists apprehended reality. The relevant term most frequently found is probably *dhamma*: this is a word of the very widest scope, as the first chapter here will show. The most awesome term is *saṁsāra*, the movement of the destinies of all living beings through incalculable aeons and universes and through multitudinous forms, until they sever the bonds binding them to time and the infatuation of mortality, and attain to freedom. The Pāli word for freedom is *vimutti*; and it is the most meaningful, as it is the most emphasized, equivalent of *nibbāna*,* the goal of Buddhist life. Vimutti is a more radical idea than we normally associate with the word 'freedom'. Its rationale is that ordinary men and women are not in control of their lives at any level, have little say in their own destinies, but can change this if they will, however great or subtle the forces normally controlling and moving them unawares.

---

* This is the Pāli form of the better-known Sanskrit word *nirvāṇa*.

In the quest for freedom, nature as denoted by saṁsāra is to be transcended. As denoted by dhamma it is to be understood, in a particular way.

Buddhism like any of the great religions is a vast and complex system. It is nonetheless reducible to a single oft-repeated statement of the Buddha: Two things only do I teach – dukkha and the ending of dukkha. This word is usually translated as 'sorrow' or 'suffering'. It is in fact nothing less than the human – and animal – state, conditioned by time and space and all the other factors that shape our lives. Wherever there is conditioned life in the universe it may be said that there inevitably is dukkha. Dukkha is saṁsāra in its inmost being. The ending of dukkha is nibbāna, a state beyond conditions and almost beyond the range of language, as it can only be suggested in negative terms – 'not born, not become, not made, not compounded, neither this world nor a world beyond'.* Nibbāna is, however, described in the Canon as a dhamma, as nature is. The antithesis is not absolute.

There are several other terms touching on the concept of nature. The simplest is probably *loka*, the world in its physical aspect; the most troublesome, *bhava*. Bhava, especially when combined with another difficult doctrinal term, *āsava*, means the deep-rooted will to keep going on in the round of saṁsāra. It is grouped with the āsavas of ignorance and appetite, and the will denoted is not so much a personal quality as a powerful, impersonal grip to be broken.

But this is an entirely different thing from the conquest of external nature in which mankind has been engaged since the beginning, and, in a manner of speaking, officially since the time of Francis Bacon. If vimutti means the liberation of man from nature it means no less the liberation of nature from man. In Buddhism the acknowledgement at least of the value of freedom is the first condition of all true relationships.

The relationship of man and nature is a paradoxical one. Man is both the conqueror and victim of nature. Nature has generated man and will destroy him. A very strange relationship, yet true; true, that is, in the sense of being actual. The question raised in Buddhism is whether it be

---

* 'A world beyond' in Christianity and Islam would mean heaven or paradise on the one side, hell on the other. These also are considered by Buddhism to be conditioned states, like life on earth; with a longer time span, perhaps, but not everlasting. The Buddhist idea of a place of punishment (*niraya*) is more like that of purgatory than hell, 'where the fire is not extinguished'.

true in any other sense: if it be the right relationship, the necessary, inevitable, inalterable one for ever and ever and ever. Time in a Buddhist perspective is very long. No false view holds good for ever. No failure is final. The greatest power of all is not the power of destructiveness but man's ability to change the roots of evil in himself into roots of good. There is no need here to go over the horrors of our past, present, and foreseeable treatment of the natural world, to say nothing of the treatment of our own kind. But if the wise learn from little errors, the rest of us may learn from great ones. Up to now we have bent our energies to transforming the world, and have been led to the edge of the void. It is useless to blame individuals, movements, ideas, the pressure of the past, for getting us there. The faults are in all of us and express themselves in blaming as much as in anything else. Each one has to deal with the roots of evil in the anguish of his own darkness. Early Buddhism placed no reliance on divine grace or favour. Its insight was unflinching and unflattering. But if it seems to offer long odds against success, it also believes that the possibility of good is greater than the actuality of evil, and that the means of realizing the good have been given to us.

The following pages are not only an exploration of Buddhist texts but a criticism of human destructiveness in the light of Buddhist morality as it applies to the natural world. In a lesser way they are also a criticism of the sentimentality which turns away from the destructiveness of nature. Buddhism is dedicated to seeing things as they are (*yathā-bhūtaṁ*) and sentimentality is a partial view. It may be less offensive than destructiveness, though the two often go together quite unself-consciously, but it imposes its own distortion on our view of things. The first element in the Buddha's Noble Eightfold Path is Right View and that has a close affinity with Right Knowledge. The first chapter here is devoted to this subject. It is the only part of the book which the ordinary reader, whether Buddhist or not, is likely to find difficult, the subject-matter not only being rather abstract but also involving some terms not normally found in Western epistemological discourse, some of these, necessarily, in the original Pāli, though this has been kept to a minimum.

The text on which the first chapter is based – the first sutta of the *Majjhima-Nikāya* – not only introduces the subject of Right Knowledge but it ties in with the *Aggañña Sutta* in a most important way. It is said to have been delivered as a corrective to intellectual pride just as the

Aggañña is directed against spiritual and social pride. The word 'aggañña' may be translated as 'origin' or 'beginning' or 'primary things', and indeed the notion of primacy pervades this study. As said above, Chapter 1 is devoted to the first element of the Noble Eightfold Path; Chapter 2 to non-injuriousness, the first of the Five Moralities or Precepts by which all Buddhists are supposed to live. Other chapters contain discussions of the primary images found in the literature, and of the question as to whether nature or culture is of first importance in the biography of the Buddha.

Then follows the discussion of the *Aggañña Sutta* itself. The myth is based on the idea of the involution and evolution of the cosmos over vast periods of time. This is the sort of timescale that Bible-based Western thinking rejected before the rise of astronomy and geology. It is a story of ethereal beings who still have traces in them of bad qualities sufficient to make trouble for themselves, their fellow beings, and their environment, until at length they become fully human – that is differentiated and functioning sexually – when they can set about making a just society which also has a place for people dissatisfied with convention. Readers who know something about the Hindu pantheon but not about Buddhist cosmology may be surprised at the absence of the Great Gods from the myth: no dreaming Vishnu, no dancing Shiva, no Mother Kālī, nature personified in all its fecundity and destructiveness. These gods evidently had not attained pre-eminent status in the time when the *Aggañña Sutta* was composed. But even if they had it must be doubtful whether any of them could have retained it where Buddhism prevailed, given the attitude to divinity reported of the Buddha. Good-natured deflation, not exaltation, is its keynote. The gods, great or small, are caught, as man is, in saṃsāra, but without man's sense of the passing of time. They are said to become aware that their long tenure of devahood is drawing to a close by evidence of personal decay. Sharing the same kind of being as man, although in different modes and spheres, they are not autonomous, much less creative entities, and certainly not to be feared or propitiated. Little more needs to be said about them in this book, which is mainly earthbound in its concerns. The gods are enjoying the fruits of good lives spent here, and tend to forget that even at the heart of the most carefree sphere of existence lies dukkha. With man, animals, demons, and spirits they make up one of the great divisions of nature as early Buddhism understood it. They did not make man in their image. Man, gods, and the rest are transient forms in the vicissitudes of saṁsāra. To be a god is to be happy and forgetful. To be human is to be aware of all the things which the gods forget; but not of the bad things only. The early Buddhists were aware of a freedom transcending the happiness of the gods. They knew as fully as it is possible to know that the human condition is beset with ills not to be avoided or ignored, and only to be transcended in the freedom of nibbāna. Being human meant that one had attained the form most apt for this end, the form through which nature could be saved. Confronting the sorrows of existence they were happy to be the hope of the world, the soteric form of life, embodying the means by which all reforming beings might pass beyond saṁsāra. We look for the key to the mystery, and we are the key. They knew this.

1

THE ROOT OF THE PROBLEM

IGNORANCE, KNOWLEDGE, AND WISDOM are concerns of such importance in Buddhism that it is often advisable to enter on a theme with a consideration of their significance for it. This is not to say, however, that references to them occur on every page of the Sutta Piṭaka, or that when they do they are always elaborate or extensive. On the contrary, the words denoting them are very often found in stereotyped combinations. *Avijjā* (ignorance) provides the readiest example. Its fundamental importance is stated and stressed in innumerable passages, yet there is no major discourse singly and explicitly devoted to it. While it is true to say few ideas enjoy a totally separate existence in Buddhism, or perhaps any other system of thought, any idea can be made the subject of a separate treatment. For whatever reason this does not happen in the Sutta Piṭaka in respect of these great concerns, ignorance, knowledge, and wisdom.

There is, however, one discourse that touches on all three together and in a masterly way. It is the first sutta of the *Majjhima-Nikāya*, called in fact the 'Root Discourse on Method' (*Mūlapariyāya Sutta*), and its position no less than its title reflects the importance it had for the compilers of the Canon. Like the opening sutta of the *Dīgha-Nikāya* it is a compendious work, but superior in construction and coherence, and intellectually more elevated. The first *Dīgha* sutta[*] provides a conventional if extended outline of morality; the *Mūlapariyāya* lays bare the forces in the human heart which make for good and evil. In the

---

[*] *Brahmajāla Sutta* ('The Perfect Net') DN.i.

Dīgha sutta we find a picture of the religious life of ancient India; in the other there is a picture of the world, without and within, transcending the limitations of time and place. The *Dīgha* sutta criticizes contemporary schools of thought; the *Mūlapariyāya* challenges the foundations of knowledge itself and proposes an alternative based upon spiritual values. Few things in the Buddhist or any other religious literature do so much in their way as this discourse attributed to the Buddha.

The scene is very simple and typical. The location is given – Ukkaṭṭhā, a north Indian town in the Gangetic plain where the Buddha's life was passed. He is sitting in the shade of a sāl tree, at its foot, or better, its root – the word for both is the same: *mūla*. This gives a poetic touch to the introductory passage: at the root of a great tree the Buddha tells his audience that he is going to speak on the root method (*mūlapariyāya*) of relating to things, on wise and unwise modes of knowledge. The 'things' – that is, the objects of knowledge – are designated by the term 'dhamma'. No other word in Pāli has so many significant meanings, ranging from the simplest phenomenon and sensation to the loftiest concepts and the Buddha's Message itself.* Other major meanings are Justice and the Cosmic Order. These and other great ideas are reflected in each other under the rubric of this one word.

The discourse has an abstract tone but makes use of exemplars. These are thereby brought into the abstract sphere and correspondingly endow that sphere with concreteness and actuality. They are human types and have a universal quality transcending the occasion of the sutta's utterance; they represent classes of mankind which have existed in the world at least since the time of the Buddha. They are the lay person who has heard but not heeded the Doctrine and the Buddhist monk. Each has his own mode of knowledge and each mode has its own special term. The verb *sañjānāti* is used of the unheeding layman, the *assutavant puthujjana*. It is cognate with the noun *saññā*, which denotes the intellectual faculty in the Buddhist model of man. One of the Buddha's devices for bringing Enlightenment or freedom of mind to people was to present them with alternatives to their accepted modes of thought or behaviour. He found a civilization dominated by a stupendous sense of time, one unmatched in the West before the nineteenth century; dominated likewise by the belief, at once vain and fearful, in an unchanging entity which passed from one life to another,

---

* With this meaning it has been spelt with a capital: Dhamma.

just as if, in the classic image, one put on new clothes after each night's sleep. The Buddha proposed an alternative model of man, one which was not based on the vanity of unchanging survival or the fear of annihilation. He analysed living beings into form, feelings, intelligence, behaviour, and transconsciousness.* The word here translated as 'intelligence' is 'saññā'. It denotes a faculty which everyone has in more or less degree, and whose operation is denoted by the verb sañjānāti. In the discourse here being considered, its range and power are set forth, and also its limitations.

The contrasting knowledge of the Buddhist monk is called *abhiññā*, with the corresponding verb *abhijānāti*. It is sometimes translated as 'intuition' or 'higher knowledge'. Neither of these is entirely satisfactory. 'Intuition', with its suggestion of random if brilliant insight, does not do justice to a form of knowledge which arises from unremitting discipline. On the other hand the term 'higher knowledge' has an air of esoterism about it, whereas the Buddha described his teaching as *ehipassika*, which might be rendered as 'See for yourself', and said furthermore that he was not a close-fisted teacher withholding knowledge from those who sincerely wished to know the truth of things. In the 'Root Discourse', the learner monk as well as the liberated arahant is said to have the knowledge called abhiññā, albeit in different degree.

Saññā, intelligence, is a natural faculty, abhiññā has to be won. Saññā is subject to what the Buddha called the 'bad roots' of behaviour, usually translated as greed, hatred, and delusion. More than that, in a very early verse of the Canon it is said to be the origin of spiritual retardation.† It has to be remembered that in the Buddhist view, a mode

---

* With all these terms I have given the broadest renderings of the Pāli names for the khandhas, or elements of personality. They are famously difficult to translate. My understanding of them is that the first three (*rūpa, vedanā, saññā*) are constitutive, providing the material for the activities of the fourth (*sankhārā*), which in turn determine the condition of the fifth (*viññāṇa*).

To the best of my knowledge the term 'transconsciousness' has not been used before for viññāṇa. The usual rendering is 'consciousness', with the explanation that it is the karmic element in personality, that which passes on and helps determine the form and constitution of the succeeding life. 'Transconsciousness' seems to say all this in a single word: that viññāṇa is both a property of one life and its future link with another.

One of the best discussions of the khandhas is to be found in *The Psychology of Nirvana*, by Rune E.A. Johansson.

† '*Saññānidānā hi papañcasankhā*' (Sutta Nipāta 874).

of knowing, a way of relating to the world, is not simply the outcome of ratiocination and choice, but is seen as a particular expression of the forces which inform the personality as a whole. The structure of the words saññā and sañjānāti* indicates a cumulative, descriptive, objectifying mode of knowledge, one which, unaided, lacks the insight to discern the operation of these forces and the will to deal with them; and may lack, further, the honesty to credit their existence in the knower's heart. The *Mūlapariyāya Sutta* uncompromisingly affirms that as long as self-interest, ill-will, and self-deception are allowed to dominate, the possibility of true knowledge is remote; an affirmation probably no more welcome in ancient India than one would expect it to be today, and understandably so, for no one takes kindly to the notion that his pursuit of truth is motivated by anything other than a disinterested desire to add to the sum of human knowledge and indeed of human happiness. But in the view of the early Buddhists no one could be detached and dispassionate with an unpurified mind, and only out of a pure mind could true knowledge arise, or at least out of a mind struggling to be pure. The other knowledge is inadequate to deal with reality because its competence lies in a relation with living beings which conceives of them as objects and deals with problems without due concern for consequences. Sooner or later these faults will show and, especially if the method has involved wrong actions, the consequences may be worse than the original trouble.

As said earlier, the exemplar of what might be called 'common knowledge' is the assutavant puthujjana. He is described as one who pays no heed to the Doctrine or to those who practise it. Elsewhere in the Canon this person can be virtually anyone, high or low, who has not heard the Doctrine – 'assutavant' literally means 'not having heard' and 'puthujjana' is 'the common man'. In this sutta his standing is elevated to the level of epistemological polarity over against the monk. From a roughly identifiable ordinary individual he is made a type and a symbol. In the standard translation of the 'Root Discourse' he is called 'the uninstructed average man' but this does him less than justice. His range of knowledge covers as many areas, visible and invisible, as the monk's. It is allowed, in fact, that he may know all about everything,

---

* The primary meaning of the prefix *sañ-* is 'together'; jānāti is the basic verb for 'to know'. Saññā is often translated as 'perception'. 'Awareness' and 'ideation' are other renderings, depending on the context.

including the monk's particular domain, nibbāna, according to his lights. Thus it cannot be argued that if only this or that field of knowledge were open to him he could deal properly with all. Every field is open to him and his method. The question to be asked concerns the value of the method. Then there is the further question of the fate of the objects of such knowledge, that is, the world and the beings that dwell in it, for this is the knowledge which makes for worldly power. In this sutta the unheeding person represents such knowledge – all over the world now, as then in ancient India. One might well call him the ignorant person, because, in Buddhist terms, his knowledge, for all its mighty scope, is an outcome of ignorance, avijjā.

Paṭhavī is the Pāli word for earth. The first dhamma this person is said to know about is the earth element: *paṭhaviṁ paṭhavito sañjānāti*. The phrase indicates the distinctness of the knowledge: he knows about the earth as the earth. Then follow the other three great elements, water, fire, and air, the constituents of the physical world according to the ancients. The same phrasing is used in each case. These form the first group of dhammas, or divisions of knowledge.

The next division comprises all that lives on the earth (*bhūtā*), including not only man and animals but the vegetal realm as well. With the elemental group of dhammas this completes the outline of external Nature in the *Mūlapariyāya*.

The discourse then touches on the spiritual realm, moving from nameless devas to greater gods. The early Buddhists saw nothing amiss in using the theological terminology of the culture about them. For the purpose of this study the most important level is that of the Ābhassaras or Radiant Devas. The creation story of the *Aggañña Sutta* is set among beings who have attained to this level. It should be remembered that the word 'deva' is not strictly equivalent to the word 'god' in either the Judaeo-Christian or Greco-Roman traditions. Deva life is continuous with human and animal life in saṁsāra. Its status may be quite humble and indeed vulnerable – for instance, as the spirit of a tree – or it may be at the highest levels of the pantheon. But however exalted these beings, there is no suggestion of union with them, nor of any transition from any level of devahood to nibbāna. In the 'Root Discourse' there is no mention of nibbāna at this juncture. Instead, from the far celestial reaches of saṁsāra the sutta plunges down into the spheres of inwardness, the senses and ideas.

Inwardness in the *Mūlapariyāya* is comprised in the levels of meditation called the four *jhānas*. Elsewhere in the Canon eight or nine levels are found, with nibbāna at the end. Here they are given in what may have been their original independent form. The first jhāna is the sphere of infinite space. On the evidence of Buddhist art it may also be called space without imposed boundaries. A convention of Buddhist sculpture is that the eyes of the Buddha are shown partly open, that is, not making a boundary of the eyelids between the outer and inner worlds but linking them, the objective and the subjective, and thus transcending the limitations ordinarily accepted by the mind.

From the sphere of infinite space there is a deepening to the sphere of infinite consciousness itself. Here the nature of personality is to be discovered and also its transcendence, as consciousness is left behind and the sphere of nothingness is entered. After this there is found a sphere which can only be suggested by paradox at the limits of language: neither-ideation-nor-non-ideation. It is as if consciousness, competent to deal even with a sphere beyond itself, and to give it the only possible name, that of nothingness, at last came to the limit of its resources and, lost for intelligible words, resorted to deliberate incoherence. The one who has not heeded the Doctrine may know all about these stages of meditation, as about elements, earthly forms, and devas.

It is at this point normally in the Canon that we should expect to find mention of nibbāna, the consummation of meditative practice. Not so in this sutta. Instead, there is a transition to the sensuous realm of experience. The Buddhists did not believe the senses to be confined to the body; they spoke of mind as a sense, too, along with sight, hearing, taste, touch, and smell. It may be that this helped the tradition to remain free of the tendency to dualism which has been so prevalent in Western thought.

Then follows the last group of dhammas: the three great ideas, representing the intellectual sphere, of unity, diversity, and totality. It is said that the puthujjana's knowledge embraces these also.

Finally nibbāna is mentioned, the ultimate object of knowledge. Its placing immediately after the intellectual series is appropriate in a discourse devoted to knowledge, and surely deliberate. The arrangement is, I think, unique to this discourse; as noted above, nibbāna is normally preceded by the meditational states. We are told that profane knowledge extends even to that great mystery; the formula applies as ever: *nibbānaṁ nibbānato sañjānāti*.

All of the foregoing – elements, beings, gods, meditational states, the senses, ideas, and nibbāna – are covered by the same word, 'dhamma'. Under the headings of these dhammas the Buddha gives an outline of reality as seen first from the standpoint of the assutavant puthujjana. There is a good deal more, however, about his relations with the world than the formula in three words ending with sañjānāti. To look more closely at the criticized mode of knowing, the quotation must be extended. *Paṭhaviṁ paṭhavito sañjānāti, paṭhaviṁ paṭhavito saññatvā paṭhaviṁ maññati, paṭhaviyā maññati, paṭhavito maññati, paṭhaviṁ-me ti maññati, paṭhaviṁ abhinandati; taṁ kissa hetu: apariññātaṁ tassāti vadāmi*: 'He knows earth as earth; knowing earth as earth he thinks about it in different ways; finally he thinks, It is mine, and exults over it. Why is this? He does not know in the fullest sense, I say.' Thus knowing in the mode of sañjānāti is succeeded by thinking from different angles, as is indicated by the variety of inflexions to which paṭhavī (and every subsequent dhamma) is subjected. An epistemic relationship is presented which appears to be entirely intellectual, entirely harmless. The great elements, or as we might call them today, natural resources, are not plundered; no living beings are killed or otherwise abused. A programme of pure intellect is presented: to know what is to be known and to think in all possible ways about the objects of knowledge. Yet, says the Buddha, all this is insufficient. Almost imperceptibly, as it seems, there is a movement from knowledge and thought to something else: *paṭhaviṁ-me ti maññati*: the earth is mine, he thinks. Knowledge has become power, or the thought of power, of possession. The movement proceeds from this to the pleasure of power and possession: *paṭhaviṁ abhinandati*; all things give joy only as things possessed. A vicious circle is seen to be established on the basis of a knowledge by which man relates falsely to the world and to all that lives in it. Why? The Buddha says in effect that the puthujjana knows no better. He has not, in the sañjānāti mode of knowledge, the means of knowing anything in all its aspects, interrelations, and consequences; he may not even have the means of knowing the inherent defects of sañjānāti, which, emphatically outward-looking, is not self-critical. When its practitioner ought to be questioning its validity and his own acceptance of it, he is found to be rejoicing in its imperfect triumphs, without unease before their consequences.

Merely to say that the practitioner of unenlightened knowledge knows no better would not by itself take the argument very far. It is

Merely to say that the practitioner of unenlightened knowledge knows no better would not by itself take the argument very far. It is necessary to know why he knows no better. In the second part of the discourse the Buddha explains. The cause lies deeper than knowledge.

The figure brought into contrast with the exemplar of ignorance is the Buddhist monk, whose mode of knowing is abhijānāti. There are gradations in the command of abhijānāti corresponding to the spiritual status of the monks, divided into learners and arahants, those monks who have lived the Buddhist life to perfection. The Buddha's words to the learner are cautionary; the right mode of knowledge is not of itself an assurance that he may not fall into wrong ways. He ought not to think about the objects of knowledge from any angle and ought not to rejoice over what he knows, even though he knows it rightly. He ought not to say of anything, It is mine, it exists for me. If he does, the good work of right knowledge will be impaired if not undone and the wrong relationship with things may be re-established, that is, the relationship which obtained when the learner was himself a puthujjana and had not joined the Buddhist community. At the end of this section, the Buddha says, by way of explanation of his cautions to the learner: *pariññeyyaṁ tassāti vadāmi*, I say he does not yet know fully. By this he indicates that there is a kind of knowledge more advanced than abhiññā though continuous with it. This is *pariññā*. Neither the learner monk nor the puthujjana has it; but the former, if he persists in the way of life he has entered, will attain it in time; not so the latter, so long as he remains unheeding of the better way.

The goal of the Buddhist monastic life was the spiritual state called *arahatta*, those who achieved it being called arahants. In the early days, especially from direct contact with the Buddha, it was a state achieved by many, we are told. More than the learner monk, in the *Mūlapariyāya Sutta* it is the arahant who is the polar opposite of the unheedful person. He is a free man in the most profound sense – free of the hold of ignorance, attachment, aversion, appetite, and even the desire for life itself. This freedom is attributed not to indifference or apathy, but to the highest wisdom, *sammadaññā*. There is no need for the Buddha to utter cautions to him. The arahant knows rightly (*abhijānāti*); he does not need to think about things from any angle nor does he rejoice over what he knows or lay claim to it. *Pariññātaṁ tassāti*, says the Buddha: the arahant knows in the fullest sense, having won to pariññā. How does this come about? the Buddha then asks, and answering his own question declares that the arahant has destroyed the roots of self-interest, ill-will, and delusion in himself.*

This is the crucial thing, according to the *Mūlapariyāya Sutta*. Only those who are conscious of the evil rooted in themselves and who strive to eradicate it can even begin to cultivate right knowledge and thereby to enter into a right relationship with the world. Success in this very difficult undertaking means right knowledge in all its fullness, that is, pariññā. But even the first steps of the learner are on the right path, if he will but keep steadfastly to the method laid down by the Buddha. The greatness of the final attainment flings its light back on the first step of all in the Buddhist life, the entry upon the path, and the first step is seen to be the most important step of all.

The dynamic of the *Mūlapariyāya Sutta* requires the rhetorical polarization of arahant and puthujjana, but the two figures are so far apart that their symbolic status predominates over all else, and the possibility of bringing them together in a meaningful way seems to be very remote.

What then is to be done? – for assuredly something needs to be done, otherwise we are left with an almost Augustinian division of mankind. This, happily, is an unfounded apprehension, for as the arahant was once a learner monk, so the latter was once a puthujjana, perhaps even a heedless one. A change from wrong to right knowledge has to be brought about; in the terms of the Noble Eightfold Path, a change from wrong to right view: *sammādiṭṭhi*, the first stage on the Path.

In the Pāli Canon, this inner transformation is usually brought about by means of a personal encounter with the Buddha or with one of his disciples. To the man or woman who comes with problem or challenge the principles of the Dhamma are set forth in a manner deemed appropriate to the person and the occasion; hopefully he or she will see their meaning and value and determine to live in accordance with

* There is a final section which purports to deal with the Buddha's own knowledge. One is diffident in commenting on anything which claims to deal with the inner life of one who, elsewhere in the Canon, is said to be beyond definition. Here we read that the Buddha's mode of knowledge is the same as the learner's and the arahant's, that is, abhijānāti. Like the arahant he knows fully but does not rejoice over it. The reason given is different, however. The three roots of unenlightened knowledge are not mentioned. Instead there is a statement about the very root of dukkha itself. It is said to be *nandī*, a synonym of *taṇhā*, craving, desire. The Buddha is said to know that this is the root of dukkha, and to have got rid of it in all its forms and thus attained to supreme wisdom.

them. The repentance of King Ajātasattu is probably the most vivid of many instances. Ajātasattu ruled over the powerful and expanding kingdom of Magadha, south of the Ganges. An ambitious man, he was also thoroughly ruthless. To gain the throne he had killed his own father, a friend and patron of the Buddha; and indeed he supported Devadatta in his bid to oust the Buddha and take over the leadership of the Order. But withal Ajātasattu was, like so many of his contemporaries, a seeker after wisdom and truth. He went from one to another of the great sages of the day and questioned them all. It was not until he had heard and pondered all the sages' counsel, some of it startlingly extreme, that Ajātasattu came at last to the Buddha. What he heard that night in a forest grove he may have heard before when the Buddha was a guest in his father's halls; only this time the words strike home and the parricide's heart is touched and he repents and determines to reform. From being a heedless puthujjana he becomes an *ariyasāvaka*, one who has heard and heeded the Dhamma. A radical change of view has been brought about. Ajātasattu, perhaps from earlier meetings with the Buddha, has at least known that something is deeply wrong with himself. He is not entirely devoid of self-criticism, but lacks the inner resources to implement it and change the life he leads. Ajātasattu is a classic example of greed, hatred, and delusion in operation. Usurper and expansionist, his motto might well be 'It is mine, it exists for me.' In Buddhist terms, his life and his mode of knowledge are inseparable; but a process of transformation can be effected even in the hardest of hearts, when the time is right.

The critical attitude essential to a system so insistent on right knowledge arises out of the Buddha's own career; indeed it antedates Gotama's attainment of Buddhahood. The going forth 'from home into homelessness' is itself a symbol of the interrogatory spirit, issuing as it does from critical dissatisfaction with the conventional possibilities of existence and career open to a young man at that time in India. Then there is Gotama's separation from his famous teachers Āḷāra Kālāma and Uddaka Rāmaputta, each in turn queried and found wanting. This part of his career is a painful interrogation of life and experience.

After the Enlightenment, the Buddha continues to question, only now as a teacher, one whose questioning can help the people who come to him, puthujjanas from all walks of life and all levels of society. What brings these people is dissatisfaction with themselves and the lives they lead. They have already taken the first step in self-criticism. The

Buddha has known their dissatisfaction. He has the authority not only of wisdom but experience. Not everyone can accept the Teaching. But of those who do, many develop the new faculty of abhiññā and go on to freedom.

The *Mūlapariyāya Sutta* is the most radical and general example of the critical attitude in early Buddhist literature. The roots of knowledge, right and wrong, are not, it says, epistemic in the final analysis but moral. Yet there is no condemnation of the assutavant puthujjana. The only judgement passed on him is *apariññātaṁ tassāti vadāmi:* not 'he is wicked', but 'he does not fully understand'.

What this tells is that even from an abstract epistemological discourse, compassion is not absent. Nonetheless, to point this out is not to lose sight of the sternness of the analysis. The assutavant puthujjana's knowledge is vitiated by surrender to the urge to power and possessiveness. A relationship based on power denies to both parties the possibility of freedom. It is thus, in Buddhist terms, an utterly false relationship. The equation of knowledge and power is the Baconian position, one from which science is only now perhaps beginning to shift. In criticizing this position, Buddhism is criticizing science; not the superseded practices of Bacon himself only; not the benefits of science as such; but the methods and presuppositions of science as inaugurated by the Baconian apologetic, and diffused and refined from then to our time and into the future. It criticizes us for accepting the benefits without regard to the methods; for not challenging the characters of our benefactors; for disregarding the self-interest, ill-will, and delusion in their hearts and in our own.

The relations of an individual or a society with the environing world are based on the kind of knowledge regulative at the time. It influences every aspect of life – attitudes, values, sympathies, the sense of obligation and the sense of responsibility. No one can deny that our relations with the world today are based on knowledge of the accumulative, power-loving kind, its greatest and most prestigious instruments being the sciences. At a very deep level we have made an act of faith in this kind of knowledge. We attribute our happiness to it and have given it charge of the future. If as at present, under threat of destruction, we have misgivings, they are rather about misapplication of the knowledge than about its assumptions, methods, and rationale. How hard a task lies ahead has been well indicated by L.C. Knights in his essay on

'Bacon and the Seventeenth-Century Dissociation of Sensibility'.* Writing of the transition from the Renaissance to the seventeenth century, which 'has long been recognized as marking in some way the beginning of "the modern world"', he says it was 'a transition that took place not only in the spheres of practical achievement and conscious intellect but in those more subtle and more profound modes of perceiving and feeling that underlie men's conscious philosophies and explicit attitudes, and that have become so ingrained and habitual that it is only by a deliberate effort of the intelligence that we can recognize them as *not* inevitable, absolute and unchanging, the permanent *donnés* of "human nature"'. This is surely true. Yet to a Buddhist the continuity of the modern period with the Renaissance is even more obvious than the disjunction, and similarly that of the Renaissance and the medieval period. None of these times is really out of joint with the next. There are stresses and strains, but they never come apart, for what unites them is never challenged, only modified and adjusted to changing circumstances. What a Buddhist sees is a tradition, not a Judaeo-Christian tradition, only, but one with a powerful Greek element, which has consistently excluded nature from ethical concern. Put crudely, he sees a clear line from the cursing of the serpent and the drowning of the Gadarene swine to the horrors of our laboratories and the extermination of species in the wild. He also sees the figure of Prometheus, the titan who stole fire from heaven and with it a light that may be less enlightening than we have hitherto believed. There is no such figure in Buddhist mythology.

Unfortunately all too many Buddhists today believe that the future of their religion is convergent with the future of science. How often has one heard and read that Buddhism is a scientific religion, the most scientific religion no less, and that this or that new theory bears out some ancient insight. It may be that there are parallels and similarities between the two; some may be important and worth a deal of co-operative investigation. Nevertheless, the assimilation of Buddhism and science is fraught with perplexity. It necessitates the most earnest questioning on the part of believers. As I have said, Buddhism is a critical discipline, and to be true to itself it must ask uncomfortable questions in every age. It has not always done so and it is not everywhere doing so today. There is no need for examples. The merest glance

* L.C. Knights, *Explorations*, p.93.

at supposedly Buddhist societies reveals unwholesome compromise of ideals and values on every side. *Corruptio optimi pessima.* It is a very sad picture. Of course there is much in it to evoke sympathy. The penetration of Buddhist countries by the Western entrepreneurial and later the colonial powers coincided with the rise of the scientific spirit and the expansion of Christianity. Their economic, political, and religious bases were attacked together. We should perhaps rather be surprised that so much has been saved.[*]

In our society, the potential value of Buddhism is that it gives a vantage point providing an overview of Western attitudes, all the clearer for being so different from virtually every body of thought or doctrine the West has produced. Writing almost a hundred years ago, Henry Clarke Warren remarked on 'the strangeness of what I may call the intellectual landscape', in which 'all the ideas, the modes of argument, even the postulates assumed and not argued about, have always seemed so strange, so different from anything to which I have been accustomed, that I feel all the time as though walking in fairyland.'[†] The strangeness may have lost some of its magic by now, yet the real mystery remains, for all the literature designed to make it better known, and the interest of men such as Whitehead and Heidegger in some of its ideas. The Buddhist position still is different from any system we have. From that viewpoint *they* all present a strange intellectual landscape and their 'postulates assumed and not argued about' are seen at last to be questionable. The strength of the position is founded on the quality of the Buddha's vision and the integrity of his system. In virtue of these the tradition he initiated can claim an honourable place in any dialogue on 'questions of ultimate concern', and on the perhaps more important penultimate and antepenultimate ones

---

[*] It has to be remarked that the Christian missionary has often had more in common with the white hunter than with his counterpart in religion, the Buddhist monk, even in these stewardship-conscious times. Travellers of an earlier generation used to be touched by the concern of individual Buddhists for domestic animals and enchanted by the tameness of wild animals in Buddhist countries. But, as Sangharakshita observes, 'the aggressive materialism of the West makes terrible inroads' into all this. 'One of the saddest sights the author has ever seen is a Roman Catholic missionary priest taking a jeep-load of Buddhist boys, all armed with rifles, for a day's "sport" in the woods. One trembles at the shocking indifference of the parents of these boys – and there are millions like them all over Asia – who unthinkingly deliver their children for "education" into the hands of the enemies of Buddhism.' *A Survey of Buddhism*, p.465.

[†] *Buddhism in Translations*, p.284.

also. Not that any such dialogue could be easy, given the Buddhist insistence on purity of heart in the development and application of knowledge. As said before, the Buddhist criticism of wrong knowledge is fundamentally a moral criticism; its epistemology is grounded in ethical priorities. To these it is now time to turn.

Before doing so, however, a final word should be said about an aspect of the 'Root Discourse' not considered before: its audience. The text simply tells that they were monks who were gladdened by the Buddha's words and rejoiced. This is the usual way of bringing a discourse to a close. But the commentary tells a different story. It says that the immediate purpose for which the Buddha preached this sutta was to dispel the conceit of five hundred monks who were proud of their theoretical knowledge of the Doctrine. It also says that they were formerly brahmans well versed in the three Vedas. This is interesting in that it touches on the relationship of wrong thinking and intellectual pride. Pride and its effects form one of the major themes of the Buddhist cosmological myth, which is also delivered to brahmans.

In addition the commentary makes it clear that monks are not automatically endowed with right knowledge by virtue simply of their calling. Left to their own devices they may be closer to the 'learned ignorance' of the assutavant puthujjana than to the liberating wisdom of the arahant. Indeed, the learner monk, sincere and strenuous, may be closer to the truth of things than they. However, if the audience of the 'Root Discourse' really did consist of monkish puthujjanas, then its value is surely enhanced, for it may be said to speak to erring seekers in all ages, lay as well as ordained, female as well as male. We know from the Canon that nuns attained to liberation; as this presupposes right knowledge and insight it cannot be said that the message of the sutta is limited to men. We also know that layfolk won release; thus the message is not confined to the Order. The laity did not have the continuous opportunity of the religious for the practice of the Dhamma in all its fullness, but they had taken the first and most important step in joining the community at large, and every effort to put the basic ethical precepts into practice meant a blow struck at the roots of evil, and an aid to the growth of goodness and to the disposition required for right knowledge and insight.

2

THE FIRST PRINCIPLE OF BUDDHISM

THE GOAL OF BUDDHISM is nibbāna, synonymous with freedom and equated with the destruction of rāga, dosa, and moha. The whole Buddhist discipline is directed to this end, a discipline founded on five resolutions which the Buddha required of every individual who accepted his teaching as a guide to life. These resolutions are the Pañca Sīla, or Five Moralities:
   (1) to refrain from taking the life of any living being
   (2) to refrain from taking anything that has not been given
   (3) to refrain from sensual misbehaviour
   (4) to refrain from false speech
   (5) to refrain from substances that induce intoxication or sloth.
The order of the Pañca Sīla tells a great deal about the priorities of early Buddhism. The first is non-destructiveness. It is the key to our relations with the world and our fellow man; more important than relations with our fellow man alone, under the headings of property, pleasure, and speech; and with ourselves alone under the heading of intemperance. If, as is proposed in this study, ethics and morality are the fundamentals of Buddhism, then it is not too much to say that the first sīla is its most important single fact. The most striking testimony to this is found in one of the mythical discourses of the Long Collection, the 'Lion-Roar on the Turning of the Wheel' (Cakkavatti-Sīhanāda Sutta, DN.xxvi), of which Rhys Davids wrote that 'Never before in the history of the world had this principle [of the Reign of Law] been proclaimed in so thorough-going and uncompromising a way.' The discourse tells, among other things, of the breakdown of society, anticipating in a

curiously precise manner Hobbes's famous dictum, for the culmination of the chaos is that people look on their fellow men as wild beasts and kill one another; and life is gradually reduced to something 'solitary, poor, nasty, brutish, and short'.

The turning point comes when they resolve to stop killing; then they go into the jungle and live on roots and fruits for seven days, at the end of which they embrace each other and there is no more killing. A new society begins, founded on non-violence, as the first Buddhist precept is reinstated. Without this it is not too much to say that the integrity of the Dhamma is so compromised as to be virtually set at nought.[*]

Inevitably a contrast with the Ten Commandments is suggested. They are not only different in their order of priorities but in what might be termed their expectations of man. In the Decalogue, man is the recipient of commands from God; in the Pañca Sīla he sets out alone to do good. A profoundly different view of man finds expression in each of the two codes. In Buddhism man is a being who can resolve of himself to lead a certain kind of life and put the resolve into practice. He is in the fullest sense an intentional being. The forces which would prevent him leading this life are situated in himself, and he can overcome them. This distinguishes Buddhism as much from conventional humanism as from conventional theism. It is as far from the hubristic tendencies of the one as it is from the prostrative tendencies of the other, nor does it swing between the two types of confidence they represent, that of pride and that of submission. In conventional theism nature is set over against God as the womb of idols; in conventional humanism nature is set over against man as the source of illness, ageing, and death. The positions are not essentially dissimilar; they are each dualistic and oppositional. The splendours of nature chiefly serve to display the power of God, as the mysteries of nature serve to display the ingenuity of man, who unriddles them. But Buddhism has its own form of humanism, just as it has its own form of theism. The *Mūlapariyāya Sutta* places man the knower at the centre of things, with all the spheres of existence open to his knowledge. In one sense the most wretched of beings in that he alone may see the dukkha of the world in something of its fullness and intensity, such that, like the Buddha himself, he may have compassion for a drop of water, man is also the most fortunate of

---

[*] In this discourse the value of the wilderness, of nature, in the healing of human ills is powerfully affirmed. See also below, Chapter 5.

beings, more so than the time-forgetting gods, in having the motivation to transcend saṁsāra. The people to whom the Buddha spoke lived in a polytheistic society. Those who took the message to heart would find no reason in it to retain any of those gods as an object or ideal of worship. Effort and not worship is the characteristic Buddhist activity, effort primarily on one's own human nature and existence. Accordingly, the first Buddhist commandment is not theological but anthropological, and reflects the belief that man is at every moment free to choose his way of life; he has in him, in spite of powerful forces pressing to determine his destiny, the capacity to respond to a call to ultimate freedom. As said above, man in the Buddhist view is an intentional being, capable of embodying an intentional ethic. In passing, it must be said that this view is the direct opposite of a great deal of Western psychology, much of which takes its tone from Freud, who said: 'It is impossible to think of a number, or even of a name, of one's own free will.' The helplessness alleged of man before a god or before the unconscious is totally at variance with the Buddhist view.

Continuing the comparison of the two codes, it is notable too that in the Pañca Sīla there is no mention of a sabbath day, sanctified by God. The early Buddhists did have a holy day, the *uposatha*, but it derives not from a creation story but from Vedic ritual, its title corresponding to that of the day of preparation before the soma sacrifice.* By the Buddha's time, the word had come to mean the days preceding the stages of the moon's waxing and waning, the first, eighth, fifteenth, and twenty-third nights of the lunar month. Pre-buddhistic reforming groups made use of these times for the expounding of their views, and the practice was continued by the Buddhists, who held a chapter of the Order on the fifteenth day of the half-month to set forth the new doctrine. At these meetings there was also opportunity for the laity to participate, renewing their resolutions as they thought about the way of the arahants: how these refrain from taking the life of any creature; how they live considerately and kindly, with compassion and mercy for all beings, never using violence against them. The lay disciple vows that during this night and day he too will refrain from taking life and

---

* The soma plant 'appears to have grown in the Himalayas and ... to judge from the hymns addressed to it in the Rig-Veda must have produced results not unlike those described by Mr Huxley in *The Doors of Perception.*' R.C. Zaehner, *Mysticism Sacred and Profane*, p.3.

will be compassionate and merciful.

The same promise is made in respect of the other sīlas, and in addition the ariyasāvaka resolves not to eat more than one full meal that day, not to dress up and go to an entertainment, and not to sleep in a luxurious bed. Thus the uposatha serves as a reminder to the laity of their responsibilities as Buddhists, reinforcing the Pañca Sīla and adding to it; but it is not raised to so exalted a place as to magnetize all goodness to itself. A poem in the *Majjhima-Nikāya* brings this out clearly. Having said that ritual bathing does not cleanse the transgressor of his evil deeds, the Buddha goes on:

> To the pure every day is holy: an uposatha,
> A day of observance to those who do good.
> So bathe in this wise, brahman: Make peace among all beings,
> Harming nought that draws breath, telling no lies,
> Taking nothing not given, having faith, being generous.'*

The uposatha marks the rhythm and passage of time as manifested by the moon. It relates the good life to the natural world, while showing its superiority to all natural forces, symbolized by light and darkness, whose continuity is emphasized rather than their contrast. They are continuous and complementary, not oppositional; neither is night symbolical of evil, even in the last phase of the moon. Uposatha is proposed as an aid in the moral life; in itself it symbolizes the transfiguration of the everyday.

Though there are many references in the Canon to the devotion of a mother to her child, there is no specific precept about the honour due to parents. In the simple terms of the Pañca Sīla, they have the same rights as other beings, that is, the right to be treated with kindness and compassion, and without violence to their persons or their feelings. This, however, indicates only the minimal duty to them. A more elaborate code of behaviour is set out in the *Sigālovāda Sutta* (DN.xxxi), called after the young family man to whom it was spoken. This Sigāla is found worshipping the six directions when the Buddha meets him. Although he is doing so on his late father's instructions, the Buddha has no hesitation in showing him a better way, the directions being made to signify his various relationships. Thus duties to parents and ancestors are given in relation with the east, whence comes the new day and new

* *Vatthūpama Sutta* MN.vii.

life. The layman should say, 'They looked after me. I will look after them. I will keep up the good customs of the family. I will be worthy of my inheritance and will honour their memory.' But these duties do not override all others; Sigāla is a husband and a father too and his duties in that direction are no less clearly spelt out. And indeed there is an area of beneficence above all family ties, for at the zenith are the services which the laity can render to those who lead the religious life; it is all too easy, all too *natural*, to set the highest value on hearth and home. Continuing the directional theme, the nadir stands for servants and workmen and all those *under*; they too have their rights as well as duties; the relations between employer and employee are based on mutual respect and friendliness. The other two directions are considered in connection with teachers and friends.

In all this there is no suggestion that affections are diluted. Parents are not loved less for not being loved exclusively. There is enough love for all and to spare. One of the strongest assumptions of Buddhism is the generative power of mind. Mind is conceived of as a sort of living fountain or well which may be drawn on inexhaustibly. This is most unequivocally attested in the meditational practice of the Four Sublime States in which one pervades the whole world with good feelings. Buddhism is an inclusive religion. Where it meets boundaries it tends to overflow or to pass round them. This may go some way to explain its tendency to syncretism, which some have found perplexing and even offensive: it may actually be no more than the inevitable effect of loving-kindness (*mettā*) and compassion (*karuṇā*). In the Buddha's day the caste system was already a subject of contention, with the brahmans asserting that they, born, as they said, of Brahmā's mouth, his words made flesh, should have the highest place in society, and that, as one of them reminded the Buddha, it was the duty of the rest to serve them. Early Buddhism was critical of this outlook, based as it is on self-interest, ill-will, and delusion. The depth of its criticism can be gauged from the myth of the *Aggañña Sutta*, the primary purpose of which was the refutation of the brahmans' claims.

It is not until the commandment against killing is reached in the Decalogue that the Buddhist and Judaic codes begin to converge; and even then the differences are as great as the similarities, for the Judaeo-Christian prohibition is confined to human beings, while the Buddha's covers all living beings.

The Ten Commandments are believed to have been given by the god Yahweh to Moses, leader of the Hebrew people. The basis of Buddhism is the Buddha's Enlightenment, his experience of nibbāna or freedom. On this rests the authority of his ethic. Stressing the analytical nature of the Enlightenment, Trevor Ling reminds us that the mind which attained it was

> essentially a mind purified, calmed, and cooled from all evil passion. It would be incorrect to say that this was merely an intellectual approach, for moral values obviously play a primary and absolutely indispensable part, too. Even so, in the last resort, Buddhist wisdom is to be regarded as a discovery of the human mind; it is in no sense a revelation to Gotama given by a non-human spirit or divine being.*

The Canon has a number of passages which describe the Enlightenment and indicate the nature of nibbāna. Most of them are fairly well known and need not be discussed here, though some of them will be touched on in a later chapter. There is, however, a comparatively unexamined sutta which throws a special light on the Buddha's experience, and on the authority deriving from it.

The Pāli language is rich in words for 'time'. This is only to be expected, perhaps, as the language is part of a culture with a powerful if not an overpowering sense of the vastness of time. Probably the most important terms are *kāla* and *samaya*. The former is the more poetic and suggestive. It means darkness also. In Hinduism it is personified as Kālī, the Black Mother, womb and mouth, generating and devouring all that lives. In Buddhism, kāla is most notable for its negative adjective, used to describe the Buddha's doctrine in the phrase *akālika Dhamma*: the doctrine free of time. But it is in terms of the more prosaic samaya that human freedom is discussed in the sutta referred to above, the 'Greater Discourse on the Simile of the Pith' (*Mahāsāropama Sutta*, MN.xxix.)

It compares the quest for truth with the efforts to get at and gain the pith of a tree. Its moral is the danger of spiritual pride. The first seeker who goes forth in faith is lauded and honoured for his efforts and in consequence he becomes arrogant to others; he resembles a man who takes the branches and leaves for the pith of the tree. Another attains to moral living, another still to knowledge and insight before succumbing

---

* *The Buddha*, p.133.

to conceit and complacency. Then there is the seeker who wins release and freedom from the things of time (*samayavimutti*). But this state, too, may be lost, even though the one who gained it is free of spiritual pride. Finally there is the seeker gone forth in faith who 'obtains release as to things that are timeless'. From the freedom associated with this (*asamayavimutti*) there is said to be no falling away.

This is the freedom the Buddha won at his Enlightenment, a state transcending both time and timelessness. There is difficulty in coming to terms with it; more than difficulty, some would say. 'It is impossible for us, constituted as we are, to escape from spatio-temporal coordinates. We cannot think in other terms, we cannot even speak the new language which would be required.' These words of the physicist F.A. Lindemann, written in the first half of the twentieth century, would probably still be echoed today.* The Buddha promised that his 'unshakeable freedom of mind' was attainable by other seekers, arahants transcending time and timelessness. Only an arahant would now be capable of refuting the physicist's assertion. Other Buddhists are in the position of all the seekers in the discourse as they set forth in faith. In the end they can only say that they accept the promise out of faith in the Buddha's word and his Enlightenment.

In the *Mahāsāropama Sutta*, the pith of the tree is gained both by the seeker released from time and the seeker released from timelessness; but only the latter state confirms the one who gains it in freedom of mind. This means that on returning from the ultimate sphere and forever thereafter he is spiritually free of the limitations of nature while living in the world; he is able to view the life of the world by a light of which he is himself an embodiment; and those who heed his message may attain to the same state and illumine the world still more with the same light. Those who describe the Buddha's message as a form of rationalism tend to ignore the transcendental element in it. The Buddha was no more an oriental Voltaire than, as A.C. Bouquet has oddly called him, an oriental John Wesley. If, as may well be said, he saw life steadily and saw it whole, it must be added that he also saw it from a suprarational viewpoint. Accordingly in the *Aggañña Sutta* the Buddha is said to have described himself as the embodiment of truth, *dhammakāya*, in the same breath as he calls himself *brahmakāya*, the embodiment of a reality mistakenly sought among the gods.

* J.W.N. Sullivan, *Limitations of Science*, p.230.

In his *Buddhist Ethics* the Venerable H. Saddhatissa writes that what in the foregoing has been called 'faith' should more properly be translated as 'confidence'. He reminds us that 'the Buddha denounced blind faith, pointing out that it is merely a form of ignorance which retards one's purification and therefore development'.* However the term is rendered, its feeling tone is certainly to be described as one of confidence: a confident belief that a way through the perplexities of life has been made available in the Dhamma. It is with this belief that the decision is made to join the Buddhist community, and the Three Refuges are invoked: first, the Buddha, as the bearer of light to a darkened world; second, the Dhamma, which is the light; third, the Sangha, the men and women who endeavour to live thereby, and to become themselves lights to the world. Taking the Refuges might be described as turning on to the path commanded by Right View; the first step on the path being the endeavour to live by the Pañca Sīla.

The Five Precepts are the means by which a start may be made in replacing the roots of evil in the heart with roots of good. They constitute an intentional ethic in the deepest sense, entailing the cultivation of altruism, goodwill, and wisdom for the eradication of self-interest, ill-will, and self-deception. They are five aspects of compassion; four of them directly, the fifth indirectly, for the disordered or slothful mind may be a source of injury whether through action or inaction. And if compassion is characterized by abstention from injury (*ahiṁsā*) it is complemented by loving-kindness, a benevolent state of mind the practice of which was believed to benefit the being on which it focused. The well-known *Mettā Sutta* conveys something of the spiritual atmosphere of early Buddhism in its attitude to the world:

> *This is what should be done by him who is wise in seeking his own good, who has gained a knowledge of the tranquil lot of Nibbāna.*
>
> *Let him be diligent, upright, and conscientious; meek, gentle, not vainglorious.*
>
> *Contented and cheerful, not oppressed with the cares of this world, not burdened with riches. Tranquil, discreet, not arrogant, not greedy for gifts.*
>
> *Let him not do any mean action for which others who are wise might reprove him. Let all creatures be happy and prosperous, let*

* Ven. H. Saddhatissa, *Buddhist Ethics*, p.54.

them be of joyful mind.

All beings that have life, be they feeble or strong, be they tall or of middle stature or short, be they minute or vast.

Seen or unseen, dwelling afar or near at hand, born or seeking birth, let all creatures be joyful.

Let no man in any place deceive another, nor let him be harsh towards any one; let him not out of anger or resentment wish ill to his neighbour.

As a mother so long as she lives watches over her child, her only child, so among all beings let boundless good will prevail.

Let good will without measure, impartial, unmixed with enmity, prevail throughout the world, above, below, around.

If a man be of this mind so long as he be awake, whether standing or walking, or sitting or lying, then is come to pass the saying, 'This place is the abode of holiness.'

He who has not embraced false doctrine, the pious man endowed with a knowledge of Nibbāna, if he conquer the love of pleasure he shall never again be born in the womb.[*]

It is to people who value the sort of relationship with the world implied here that the Buddha's message chiefly appeals. Primarily an expression of non-destructiveness or harmlessness, it corresponds with his affirmation that every living being desires the continuance of its own existence, which implies that simply in virtue of living it has the right to this desire. To the majority of people it will seem an unrealistic ideal; to the majority of living beings it is a simple impossibility, formed as they are to live by the destruction of other lives. If the ethic does not appeal to the former, it does not apply to the latter. A closer look must now be taken at this paradox of the Dhamma.

* R.C. Childers' translation of 1870, reprinted in the *Pali Buddhist Review*, vol.1, no.1, January 1976.

3

MAN AND ANIMAL

THE NATURE OF the paradox may be indicated by recalling a disagreement between the views of two pioneers of modern Buddhist studies, T.W. Rhys Davids and his wife Caroline. While his writings, especially his introductions to the suttas of the *Dīgha-Nikāya*, are still valuable, his wife's opinions are more provocative. Her idea of early Buddhism was idiosyncratic, but, expressed sincerely and repeated insistently, it was not without influence. How far her views in general coincided with those of her husband is a question which cannot be examined here. In one relevant particular, however, they seem to have been at variance. Remarking on one of the long suttas (DB.III.33), T.W. Rhys Davids wrote:

> *The mental attitude of Indians towards animals is quite different from our own. They regard animals as on a lower plane than men, but different (not in kind), only in degree. They take for granted the very real relationship between men and animals which we fail to realize, and often deny.*

Mrs Rhys Davids found this difference 'only in degree' objectionable and inevitably not part of primitive Buddhism. Perhaps because of her upbringing as a vicar's daughter in Victorian times a graduated relationship between man and animal seemed a threat to human dignity. If Buddhism did not originate the belief, she wrote, it certainly fostered it, with the result that when a decline occurred in 'the sublime worth and sanctity of the *nature* of the very man, the self, the soul, *then* the notion of reincarnation in an animal became not only not repugnant, but even plausible'.* There would seem to be echoes here of the shock of Darwinism on the beliefs of her earlier years; and the reaction against evolutionary theory may be heard, perhaps, as she goes on:

> *It is to read the new into the old to see in the notion any special*
> *Indian or Buddhist sympathy with animals as being by nature akin to*
> *man. I do not find animals included among 'beings': satta. Worth is*
> *paid to the relatively high capacity of the horse and elephant for*
> *training.... The cult of the monkey is much later.*

Satta is a more particular term than that found in the *Mūlapariyāya Sutta*. There the word used, *bhūtā*, covers not only men, gods, and animals but the vegetal realm as well. *Satta* makes a distinction, most explicitly manifested in the *Aggañña Sutta*, between forms of life which grow out of the earth and those which move freely on or over it. Among instances of the use of *satta* for animals there is one particularly revealing of Buddhist attitudes to wild creatures. It is found in a *paritta*, or invocation of goodwill, in the *Aṅguttara-Nikāya*, to be uttered for protection in the wilderness. The occasion was the death of a monk from snakebite. This happened, the Buddha is reported as saying, because the monk 'did not suffuse with heart of amity the four royal families of snakes'. He commends the following sentiments, the word *mettā*, here translated as 'friendly feelings', being repeated throughout in the Pāli. *Sattā, bhūtā*, and *pāṇā* (breathing creatures) are used synonymously for the different forms of animal life.

> *For the Virūpakkas may I have friendly feelings*
> *For the Erāpathas may I have friendly feelings*
> *For the Chabbyāputtas may I have friendly feelings*
> *For the Kaṇhagotamakas may I have friendly feelings*
> *For footless beings may I have friendly feelings*
> *For twofooted beings may I have friendly feelings*
> *For fourfooted beings may I have friendly feelings*
> *For manyfooted beings may I have friendly feelings.*
> *All beings that are and breathe and live*
> *May all be good that look on me*
> *May none be bad that meets with me.†*

* *Indian Religion and Survival*, p.46.
† AN.II.67.

The attitude is of course open to the charge of imprudence, or worse, and the charge has duly been made. In contrast, the brahman

> is not urged to love other people, especially low-caste people, only to be kind to them, to pity them, and to sympathize with them, which, indeed, may be enough. At any rate it does not expose him to the absurdity of employing his 'love' as a magical means of preventing wild beasts from hurting him, as does the Buddhist, who, when a roaring lion would attack him, simply stands still and inundates the lion with 'love', till the beast retires in confusion.*

Absurd perhaps, but all of a piece with the Buddhist ethos that the final responsibility for what befalls him rests with the individual. It is not the snake or the lion or the furious elephant which is at fault but the insufficiently loving victim; and the consequences of a poisoned, devoured, or crushed almsman would not be a hunting party but, on the part of his confrères, a greater cultivation of mettā for the killer; though not perhaps of sympathetic joy. In the Book of the Discipline, we read of a maddened elephant, set on by the evil Devadatta, charging the Buddha, who subdues him by the means which the above writer finds so unconvincing.

But no blame attaches to an animal which kills or mutilates; it is accepted that the impulses of its nature are imperative. It inhabits the realm of adhamma, that is, amorality. The starkest description of this says that 'among animals there is no living by the Dhamma, no living in peace, no doing good or meritorious deeds; they are caught up in a cycle of mutual destruction and devouring and preying on the weak.'† There are other texts which modify this extreme statement. In the *Anguttara-Nikāya* the Buddha is reported as saying that animals may be reborn not only as men but as devas; it does not happen often but it happens, and it signifies an early Buddhist belief that individual animals can transcend their worst impulses by disinterested and generous actions, and that these have a bearing on their destinies. Thus it is accepted, as it is not in other religions, that animals, though inhabiting an amoral sphere, have a moral sense and a moral capacity; and accordingly an animal may from time to time surpass its natural condition and rise above instinct to intentionality, the obscurity of its

* E. Washburn Hopkins, *Ethics of India*, p.137.
† *Bālapaṇḍita Sutta*, MN.cxxix ('On Foolish and Wise Persons').

moral sense being thereby enlightened, its consciousness gradually altered, until eventually it may emerge from pure animality and enter the freer human sphere, which offers the means of eradicating rāga, dosa, and moha and attaining to final freedom.

Man in the Pāli Canon is the soteric form in nature, the egress from time and the conditions of existence. If his being is continuous with that of animals, it is still distinct in virtue of its greater moral scope and also of its greater moral responsibility. But if the emergence of a being out of animality is a long, long process, the reverse may happen very soon, as we read in another dialogue (MN.lvii). It is said that two men came to the Buddha and asked him what their future state would be; they wished to be reborn among the devas. To this end one of them had lived as a canine, the other as a bovine ascetic, behaving to the utmost of their capacity as dogs and cattle do. This sacrifice of their human nature was intended to win the compensation of divinity in the afterlife. The Buddha, it is said, reluctantly told them that what was in store for them was likely to be very different. If they did not find themselves in purgatory (niraya), they would be reborn among the kinds of animals to whose behaviour they had habituated themselves, for beings are heirs to their deeds. Elsewhere we read: 'Various are the ways in which I might talk about the animal realm, but to convey in words its misery is far from easy' (MN.cxxix).

The two ascetics are said to have heeded the Buddha's words. Seniya, the canine, joined the Order and soon attained to arahantship; Punna, the bovine, became a lay follower. This is probably the most concrete instance in the Sutta Piṭaka of the belief in a human–animal continuum. But it can hardly be called a discordant one. The assumptions of Buddhist ontology would seem to apply, with only differences of emphasis, to both human and animal. This ontology is founded on the doctrine of the khandhas, the five elements of individuality: body, feelings, intelligence, activities, and transconsciousness.

As said earlier, my understanding of this much-discussed doctrine is that the first three elements are constitutive; that their activities make up the individual's moral nature; that this is registered by the consciousness which has an inherent faculty of judgement; that the consciousness itself is gradually modified in the process until at death, which is the disintegration of the constitutive elements and the cessation of their activities, it passes on to become the moral basis of a succeeding life. Assuming that form bodily may be the reflection of a moral judgement made in the transition from death to regeneration, and allowing the fullest latitude to the elements of feeling and mind, there would seem to be nothing in the khandha doctrine to create an impassable divide between man and beast; and so it has been understood in the tradition.

This of course is a different concept from those usually associated with religion and philosophy, in which ideas of soul and spirit play a dominant part. Those ideas create a boundary in the way we think about man and animal, enforcing a separation which evolutionary theory has if anything aggravated, through judging human intellect as the crown of evolution and the scientific attitude as the jewel in the crown. The Buddhist khandha model emphasizes what unites and not what separates. It no more denies that an animal has feelings and intelligence, however particular, than that it has a body through which to manifest them; nor does it deny that an animal's consciousness is mutable by supra-instinctive activities proceeding from its own being. The system which produced the *Mūlapariyāya Sutta* looks doubtfully at the modern pride of intellect, of which Giuseppe Tucci has written:

> *The West indeed, as though to designate its present inclinations, has coined a new word, unwonted in the history of human thought, the word 'intellectual' – as though it were possible to have a type of man reduced to pure intellect.*[*]

The extreme value set on this faculty almost inevitably encourages attitudes of superiority and exploitation towards those beings to whom it is believed to be denied.

All this being said, however, it must straightaway be affirmed that the idea of a human–animal continuum has no bearing whatever on the First Principle of Buddhism or on the allied principle of universal compassion. Whether or not the khandha doctrine is interpreted in a manner favourable to the idea, the authority of these principles is in no way impugned, for in no way do they rest on it, but on the Buddha's own order of priorities. Loving-kindness and compassion are asseverated in the Sutta Piṭaka without ontological support; their foundation is the virtue of ahiṁsā.

---

* *The Theory and Practice of the Mandala*, p.1.

This is one of the great principles of Indian religion generally, even if its most cogent formulation is in the first of the Buddhist sīlas. Its emergence, as I.B. Horner has said, is historically speaking not clear, nor can its origin be traced to any particular teacher, social reformer, or law-giver.* It is no less associated with the Jains than with the early Buddhists, and indeed the word ahiṁsā is found more insistently in Jaina scripture than in the Pāli Canon. But the principles of non-destructiveness and universal compassion are proclaimed most powerfully in certain discourses attributed to the Buddha, and, as said above, with no reference to human–animal continuity. Even a brief glance at these suttas may bring out something of the strength of feeling aroused in the early Buddhist community by animal abuse, as it was displayed in the sacrificial ritual.

The first of these suttas is the *Brāhmaṇadhammika*, found in the very ancient Sutta Nipāta. It is an appeal to the better nature of the brahman caste on behalf of the cows slain in sacrifice. The second is the perhaps better-known *Kūṭadanta Sutta* of the *Dīgha-Nikāya*; there the protest is widened to include other animals – bulls, steers, goats, rams – which ended their lives under the priestly blade. Blood-sacrifice was one of the chief offences of the age, according to the Buddha's criticism. There is in the Canon some evidence, albeit indirect, that even in his lifetime the force of this was beginning to have effect, and it would appear that with the spread of the Dhamma there came to be a change in attitudes towards animals. Certainly when, some two hundred years after the Buddha, the Emperor Asoka was converted, it was a virtually obligatory consequence that he should do as much as lay in his power to discourage all forms of animal abuse, as is shown in his famous edicts, which were carved on rock and pillar throughout the Empire.†

* *Early Buddhism and the Taking of Life*, p.3.
† Rock Edict I tells of the great slaughter of animals done for the royal kitchens, and looks to its total abolition. Pillar Edict V regulates and restricts the destruction of animals in the Empire, whatever the creed, class, or social customs of the people involved (see below p.91). Yet Theravadin Buddhism is not a vegetarian creed. Although it is laid down, both for the Order and the laity, that Buddhists must neither do nor cause the killing of any being, they are not forbidden to eat meat or fish. One of the great themes of the Pāli Canon is the danger of spiritual pride, and abstinence from meat-eating can undoubtedly lead to this in some cases. In the India of the Buddha's day, meat and fish were regular features of the popular diet, and Buddhism was a popular movement, directed towards all the castes. To have displayed choosiness in the alms-round would have been to conform to that exclusivism which the Buddha condemned in the brahmans. It would also have meant that those most likely to offer meat to the monks – butchers, trappers, hunters –

How much the traditional Indian veneration of the cow owes to the Buddha is a question which cannot be entered on here. But it is impossible to believe that the poignant poem in the Sutta Nipāta had no effect on the minds and hearts of the Buddha's countrymen. In it the Buddha tells what happens when the will to power invades the religious sphere. The poem is said to have been given as an answer to an audience of brahmans, uneasy about current practices and wishing to know if something better had once prevailed. The Buddha begins with praise of the sages of olden times:

The holy life and virtue
and temperate austerity,
likewise restraint and harmlessness
and tolerance – these they honoured.

Such sacrifices as they performed were innocent; they never shed the blood of cows, whose praise the poem now sounds:

As mother, father, brother,
or any kin whatever,
are cows; they are our best friends,
providers of our welfare:

giving nourishment and strength,
and beauty and contentment.
Knowing the truth of this,
be sure, they slew no cows.

They made sacrifices out of oil, ghee, and other harmless things. But in time, alas, this good attitude altered and brahmans grew covetous of the king's wealth and desirous of his women.* They persuaded him to allow blood-sacrifice. The victims were not only cows but horses and even men. The brahmans, although receiving gifts at the king's hands,

---

would have been denied the spiritual converse which alone might cause them to change their mode of livelihood, if that were possible in ancient India. Although trafficking in living beings was one of the trades forbidden to Buddhists, and it was said that the future lot of those who lived thereby would be hard, these were the people who stood in most need of Buddhist compassion, and to have denied it to them for the reason which created the need would have been to compromise the Buddha's social doctrine, while leaving the abuse of animals precisely as it was.

* The king is the legendary Okkāka, progenitor of the Buddha's own Sākyan people.

grew insatiable in their greed both for riches and for sacrifice. This gradually came to be concentrated on cows alone,

> *which harm not with hoof or horn,*
> *though armed like the mountain goat.*
> *Yet the gentle givers of milk*
> *were gripped by the horn*
> *and slain with the king's sword.*

So great was the slaughter that not only the gods but the titans and the demons were revolted. 'Injustice' was their cry. However, the deeds of the king and his brahmans were disastrous not only for the innocent victims but for humanity as well:

> *Once there were but three troubles:*
> *longing, want and ageing;*
> *from cruelty to animals*
> *came eight and ninety more*

> *This evil of cruelty is not*
> *of today or yesterday;*
> *where the innocent are slain,*
> *justice is degraded.*
> *So this degenerate practice*
> *is censured by the wise;*
> *those who know*
> *blame the men of blood.*

In this poem compassion for animals and denunciation of cruelty found full expression without recourse to the belief in human–animal continuity, as said above. The same is true of the *Kūṭadanta Sutta* (DN.v). The person after whom the discourse is titled is said to have been a brahman attached to King Bimbisāra of Magadha, the powerful kingdom south of the Ganges. Bimbisāra was a friend of the Buddha and a patron of the Order. But whatever he may have thought personally about the Buddha's message he was clearly not enforcing a policy of ahiṃsā on his subjects, for Kūṭadanta was preparing a considerable sacrifice. Bulls, steers, heifers, goats, and rams, in their hundreds, had been brought to the sacrificial post. But fortunately for them Kūṭadanta is not well versed in the niceties of all the rituals, and so he takes his problems to the Buddha, who, he understands, knows everything there is to know about sacrifice. What he hears in the event surpasses his expectations.

Once upon a time, the Buddha says, there was a rich and mighty king known as Mahāvijita who decided to perform a great sacrifice whereby to secure his good fortune for ever. So he summoned his chaplain, a brahman as Kūṭadanta is, to instruct him in his design. The chaplain's advice was wide-ranging, and comprised not only a survey of the ills of the royal domains, but suggestions for their cure. The king implemented these and there was peace and happiness everywhere. This is an interesting passage in its own right, as illustrating Buddhist socio-economic thinking. The chaplain – supposedly the Buddha in a previous life – says: 'The country is sorely troubled by robbers who prey on towns and villages and make the roads unsafe. This being so, it would not be right to levy a new tax on the people. On the other hand, punitive measures will not work with the robbers. Degradation, banishment, fines, imprisonment, death – these will not work: there will always be others and they will go on causing trouble. But there is a way to put an end to the disorder. Let the king give support to people in their careers and professions. The farmer, the tradesman, and the civil servant, let him give to each according to his needs, whether seed-corn or capital or adequate wages or just food. Then the various groups which constitute society will no longer produce miscreants to trouble the realm; the king's revenue will go up; and the land will be peaceful. The people will be at ease with themselves and each other, and dwell with open doors, dandling their children in their arms.'

King Mahāvijita followed the chaplain's advice and things turned out accordingly. Then at length he made his sacrifice. But it was not the sort of sacrifice that Kūṭadanta had in mind: 'At that sacrifice no oxen were slain, nor goats, nor swine nor birds nor any other living creatures. No trees were cut down to be used as posts, no grasses mown to strew around the place of sacrifice. The workers and messengers were not driven by beatings and fear; they did not work with tears on their faces. People worked or did not work as they chose, selecting their own tasks, and what they did not do was left undone. Ghee and oil, butter and milk, honey and sugar – these were what was sacrificed that day.'

The grand result is that Kūṭadanta becomes a disciple and sets free the hundreds of bulls and steers and heifers, and the hundreds of goats and rams, to eat green grass and drink fresh water, with cool breezes playing about them.

This story is really a Jātaka tale, in sutta form. But its fantasy is serious and its various points tellingly made. What is important to say here is that while compassion and non-destructiveness are commended they are not made in any way dependent upon the idea of a human–animal continuum. They are values existing in their own right at the heart of the Dhamma, independent of ontological considerations. That is not to say that such considerations are to be set aside as obsolete or too redolent of the general Indian tradition. It may be that, along with the anattā doctrine, they will form a serious part of the debate which advances in the genetic sciences are forcing on us. Some terms of the Greco-Semitic ontological tradition – nephesh, psyche, anima, nafs, soul – may have to be re-examined if lines of demarcation between man and animal are blurred, or indeed crossed, in our laboratories; this however lies outside the scope of these pages.

But before leaving the subject of animals, their place in the rich imagery of the Canon must be considered.

4

IMAGES FROM NATURE

ETHICAL FORMULATIONS REPRESENT an ideal; they show how the world would be ordered and its inhabitants made righteous and happy if this or that religion had its way. In its ethical formulations a religion is, so to say, on its best behaviour; it is also on its guard. In the imagery of its scriptures it is usually less so; not always, of course, as the figurative language, too, may be highly deliberate. In either case, it repays the closest study, as being a possible source of light on things otherwise obscure.

The general impression of the Pāli Canon in the West is of a vast, cumbersome, and repetitious collection of sermons and other gloomy sayings. It is not absolutely an erroneous impression. Repetition there certainly is, due in part, it is thought, to the suttas being delivered to a preliterate society in which repetition was the surest way of fixing the words in the hearer's memory. Some suttas, individually and in groups, were crudely put together by their editors. No one can deny that the Canon is vast. It keeps to no middle way in terms of quantity. The Old Testament, the New Testament, and the Koran are models of concision beside it. Yet the numerous volumes of the Sutta Piṭaka, the Vinaya, and the Abhidhamma, to say nothing of the Jātakas, are full of fascinating things. Not the least of these is their wonderful wealth of natural imagery, as revealing of attitudes, in its way, as ethical and philosophical statements.

In the Jātaka tales the Buddha is often represented as an animal which lays down its life to save others. In the Sutta Piṭaka there is nothing of this sort, but comparisons and likenesses abound. Some are surprising, as when the Buddha is called a tiger or, more often, a lion, which then as later was esteemed the king of beasts (*migarājā*). One of the most striking bits of imagery is in the *Aṅguttara*, where the lion's prowess is compared to the Buddha's skill as teacher of puthujjanas,[*] even those least likely to be interested in compassion for other beings; the reference is to bird-catchers who sprinkled rice on the ground as bait for their prey. To us it may seem a strange use of imagery to compare the promulgator of the first sīla with one of the great killers of the wild. The early Buddhists evidently saw nothing anomalous in it. There are other images in the Canon drawn from destructive and indeed forbidden trades, and they saw nothing strange in attributing their use to the Buddha himself. The most remarkable is probably in the 'Sutta on the Foundations of Mindfulness' (*Mahāsatipaṭṭhāna Sutta*, DN.xxii):

> *Just as if, monks, a clever cow-butcher or a cow-butcher's apprentice, having slaughtered a cow and divided it into portions, should be sitting at the junction of four high-roads, in the same way, a monk reflects on just this body, according as it is placed or disposed, by way of the material elements: 'There are, in this body, the element of earth, the element of water, the element of fire, the element of wind.'[†]*

Buddhists, in conformity with the first sīla, were unlikely to become butchers, yet the Buddha is shown as honouring the butcher's skill. It is a commonplace of Western writing about Indians, whether of ancient or modern times, that they find no trouble in holding contradictory ideas. We do not have to go so far here. Different cultures have different conventions in rhetoric and style as in everything else. And Buddhism has never been a condemnatory religion; it is more free with praise than blame, more concerned to raise than to depress. Being mentioned and thus honoured in a discourse, the butcher might be regarded in a new and better light; he at least would receive compassion from the Buddhist community even if he withheld it from his victims; but in time he might see himself as capable of a better way of life, and so might the hunter and the bird-catcher. Neither is the lion condemned for being a killer. No demerit attaches to a lion's way of life. So his prowess may be praised, as his roar is praised when used of certain utterances of the Buddha and his leading disciples, even though the roaring of a lion is described as a cause of consternation to other animals:

[*] AN.III.99.
[†] Nyāṇaponika Thera, *Satipatthana: The Heart of Buddhist Meditation*, p.130.

Monks, the lion, king of beasts, at eventide comes forth from his lair.
Having come forth from his lair he stretches himself. Having done so
he surveys the four quarters in all directions. Having done that he
utters thrice his lion's roar. Thrice having uttered his lion's roar he
sallies forth in search of prey.

Now, monks, whatever animals hear the sound of the roaring of the
lion, king of beasts, for the most part they are afraid: they fall to
quaking and trembling. Those that dwell in holes seek them:
water-dwellers make for the water: forest-dwellers enter the forest:
birds mount into the air.

Then whatsoever ruler's elephants in village, town or palace are
tethered with stout leather bonds, they burst and rend those bonds
asunder, void their excrements and in panic run to and fro. Thus
potent, monks, is the lion, king of beasts, over animals; of such mighty
power and majesty is he.*

This passage, found in the *Aṅguttara Nikāya*, is vivid and convincing.
But the description of the lion is as much emblematic as realistic.
Emblematic, too, is the Buddha's famous lion-posture (*sīhaseyyā*),
which he is said to have assumed before he died: lying on his right side,
as the animal was supposed to do, with one leg resting on the other.[†]
The Gangetic plain with its several states and growing population was
being steadily urbanized in the Buddha's time, with much clearing of
forests and destruction of habitat.[‡] Predatory animals are among those
most affected by population growth, and the people of Magadha and
Kosala and the other states would have taken steps to eliminate what
they believed to be the menace of the lion. The aristocratic pastime of
hunting for sport would have taken additional toll. This may explain
why the lion is not a living presence in the Buddha's biography, while
remaining an archetypal image of power and majesty.

The bull is another title given in honour to the Buddha; he is called
the Bull of the Sākyans and the Bull of the Stars, meaning the moon.
He himself uses the figure of the bull to illustrate the qualities of an
arahant in leading his fellow monks across the river of death, describing how a certain herdsman got his charges across the Ganges: first he
brought them to a ford; the bulls, 'the sires and leaders of the herd',

---

* David Maurice, *The Lion's Roar* (unnumbered page).
[†] See 'The Book of the Great Decease', DB part II, p.149 (*Mahāparinibbāna Sutta*, DN.xvi).
[‡] See Ling, *The Buddha*, ch.3.

went over first; they were followed by the steers and bullocks; after them came the half-grown bull-calves and heifers, then the weaker calves and finally the new-born calf with its mother. All of them signify different stages of spiritual development.* Once again there is a strangeness in the similitude. To us the bull is a symbol of sexual potency first and foremost. But it may be that to the Indians of the Buddha's day its symbolic value was quite different, so that there was nothing anomalous in bringing it into similitude with men who had transcended the instinctual life. Instinct and transcendence were more closely associated in their minds than in ours. We tend to think of instinct as subjected to repression and wish to liberate it, whereas the ancients saw themselves as subjected to the power of instinct and wished to be free of it. Our experience being of distortion and imbalance, we long for a fuller and healthier instinctual life. Such a life they enjoyed from the cradle, but in due course they wished for something better and set out to attain it. Those who idealize the instinctual life must find this strange. Even in religion, there are many today who are not at ease with the idea of transcendence.

Like the lion, however, the bull has no real physical presence in the Sutta Piṭaka, and, wild or tame, never crosses the path of arahant or novice. The one animal which has both presence and imaginal force is the elephant. All through the Canon we are reminded of how great a part this animal played in the life of ancient India. We first hear of it in the opening sutta of the *Dīgha-Nikāya*, where it is said that the multitude went to see contests between elephants, and between other animals and also birds; entertainments forbidden to the Sangha. In the second sutta the riding elephant appears when King Ajātasattu of Magadha visits the Buddha, mounted on one. Elsewhere, we read of the King Pasenadi of Kosala riding on an elephant with one of his queens before and one behind him. It is the military elephant, however, which provides the significant imagery; its control and patience and endurance made it an object of admiration, and in a couplet of great soteriological interest these words are attributed to the Buddha:

> *Victorious and free, I free others from fetters –*
> *I the elephant most controlled and skilled and calm.*[†]

---

* 'The Lesser Discourse on the Cowherd' (*Cūḷagopālaka Sutta*, MN.xxxiv).
† AN.IV.85.

The names of a few elephants have been preserved in the Canon. The most famous is Nalagiri, which at the instigation of Devadatta charged the Buddha and was subdued by his loving-kindness. The encounter is one of the favourite subjects of Buddhist art, the beast, his fury calmed, being shown on his knees before the Tathāgata.

Elsewhere in the Canon there are friendlier meetings. In the *Udāna*, for example, the story is told of how the Buddha, wearied by the throng of religious and lay people pressing in upon him, separates himself from them and goes for retreat to a forest glade. There he encounters an old bull elephant, who has similarly separated himself from the press of the herd, and they dwell there together in amity, the elephant bringing water in his trunk for the Buddha in his resting place under a sāl tree. It is a charming story and, set down by monks, is told with a refreshing irony at their own expense (*Udāna* IV.v).

There is also a Majjhima sutta in which the way of the solitary elephant is commended to the earnest seeker. The occasion here is discord in the Order. Why, asks the sutta, when bad people live in harmony, do good people quarrel, and why is it so hard to find a companion on the path? It then breaks into verse and gives this advice:

Better go on alone than be stuck with a fool;
Then do so, without doing wrong, at your own pace,
*Like an elephant, an elephant in the jungle.**

But mostly it is the tamed elephant that figures in the Canon, and they were tamed in great numbers for war, for work, and for transport; when Ajātasattu visited the Buddha he is said to have been followed by a retinue mounted on five hundred she-elephants. The elephant trainer and driver was a common figure in Indian society. We meet the son of one, a mendicant called Pessa, in the *Kandaraka Sutta* (MN.li). He remarks to the Buddha that compared with human beings, animals are 'an open clearing'. The Buddha agrees and characterizes man as the tormentor, whether of himself or of others; the good man inflicts no torment. Thus man is described, and this is rare, in terms of a single quality, the quality which arises particularly from the root of ill-will, and which it is the object of the first sīla to overcome.

* *Upakkilesa Sutta*, MN. cxxviii ('On Defilements').

Some five hundred years elapsed before the Buddha's story was told in full for the first time, in Aśvaghoṣa's *Buddhacarita*. Nothing could demonstrate the predominance of the elephant image in the tradition better than the tale of Queen Māyā's dream in the poem. She and her husband Suddhodana

> *tasted of love's delights, and one day she conceived.... Just before her conception she had a dream. A white king elephant seemed to enter her body, but without causing her any pain. So Maya, queen of that god-like king, bore in her womb the glory of his dynasty.* *

For all that, however, the course of the Buddha's life is associated less with elephants and other animals than with trees. His birth, Enlightenment, and death all took place in the shadow of trees and the Dhamma was often taught at their foot, as in the *Mūlapariyāya Sutta*. More than once the Buddha says that if the great sāl trees round about had understanding they would give assent to what he had just expounded. Trees, although classed among the beings, bhūtā, of the *Mūlapariyāya*, were not sattā like men and animals; indeed the word for the vegetal realm is *bhūtagāma*. They are said to be without consciousness, but to have resident spirits (*devatā*). These were capable of feeling distress and at such times other devatās might leave their abodes in trees and herbs and grasses and come to offer solace. In a Majjhima sutta there is a sāl tree whose devatā is thrown into a state of great anxiety because a seed-pod of a creeper is threatening the tree, and with it the devatā, who seems powerless to do anything about the danger. It is as if spirits of vegetation were believed to share the passive nature of their hosts. Even those who come to comfort him can do nothing. They can only urge him not to be afraid, for a bird or a deer or ants may eat the seed, or it may be removed by woodmen or destroyed by fire or it may not germinate. This is the limit of their helpfulness.

How seriously the early Buddhists took these dryads and their herbal kin it is not possible to say with certainty. The above story is not there in its own right but as a similitude for the dangers of sensuality, represented by the 'young, soft, and downy arms' of female religious mendicants. It may be no more than an instance of the homiletic use of folklore, and have little or nothing to do with belief. Certainly we do not find the early Buddhists offering prayer to these or to higher spirits,

* E. Conze, *Buddhist Scriptures*, p.35.

as Socrates prayed to Pan and his fellow gods. Yet they shared the culture of their neighbours and no violent rupture with it was enjoined on them. If they maintained a critical detachment, it was not unsympathetic to the ways of the common man, and the impulse, exemplified in the *Sigālovāda Sutta*, was towards spiritualization and not denial. Belief or disbelief in dryads and naiads was no bar to doing good and gaining merit. As there are passages in which devatās are mentioned, so there are passages in which they are not. In the *Saṁyutta-Nikāya* we read how great trees overshadow smaller trees, which gradually decline and fall to the ground. Here once again is the conventional metaphor of desire overpowering virtue; but there is no mention of devatās. This suggests that the early Buddhists had distanced themselves from the prevailing animism, and could, when desirable, discourse without using a mode of speech qualified thereby. When the Buddha remarks that the surrounding sāl trees would give assent if they had understanding, there is no reference to resident spirits. In a *Dīgha* sutta it is said that most spirits did not believe in the Buddha; the reverse may also have been true.

'I am very weary, Ānanda, and would lie down,' says the Buddha to the companion of his last days on earth, requesting him to prepare a place between two sāl trees. There, near the small township of Kusinārā in the land of the Mallas he passed away. Later it came to be a matter of acute embarrassment to the Buddhist community, now thriving and status-conscious, that the Master had chosen so humble a place to die, and they made up a fable, touchingly vulgar and inflated, about the former glories of the spot, whose name was also upgraded to Kusāvatī, and of its king the great Suddassana, supposedly a previous life of the Buddha. They so far forgot themselves and the priorities of the faith as to make their ideal ruler a hunter's dream and a conservationist's nightmare, endowing him with eighty-four thousand chariots covered with the skins of lions, tigers, and panthers, and with a palace whose divans were covered with long-haired rugs and antelope skins, to say nothing of the ivory which went into their making. The list is given no less than three times in the *Mahāsuddassana Sutta*. Uncritical grandiosity could hardly go much further. It is as close to impiety as piety can go. But whatever they might add to the narrative of the Buddha's death, they could not remove what was already there; and the weariness and the final resting place between the trees remain as first recorded, both convincing and moving in their simplicity.

The Enlightenment is also described as taking place under a tree. 'Accompanied only by his resolution', writes Aśvaghoṣa, 'he proceeded to the root of a sacred fig-tree, where the ground was carpeted with green grass. For he was definitely determined to win full enlightenment soon.'[*] Attacked by the army of Māra, personification of death and destructiveness, Gotama touched the earth, which 'roared and sounded forth a deep and terrible sound', and Māra's host fled in terror. The earth-touching gesture is one of the most celebrated themes in Buddhist art; the moment is one of particular interest, as it makes the earth a support and witness of good against evil. The *Buddhacarita* is a Mahāyāna poem, but the story seems to have been known to the compilers of the Sutta Piṭaka, though not developed by them.[†]

The Buddha is said to have passed the week after winning Enlightenment in meditation under the sacred fig tree. The second week was spent under a banyan tree; this tree, because of its ability to put down roots from its spreading branches, came in time to be a symbol of the spread of the Dhamma. The third week, spent under another tree, was one continuous storm, during which the serpent king Mucalinda wound his body round the Buddha, and protected him with his hood. It was at this time that Māra's daughters are said to have come and made a final unavailing attempt to move him. The last week was spent in meditation under a tree whose name or title, unusually, has come down to us. It was called Rājāyatana, meaning the King's Abode.

The Enlightenment was the culmination of years of striving. But the Buddha's spiritual experiences are not to be confined to these years, nor does the striving with its austerities entirely account for the final triumph. When brought to the extreme of suffering by his mortifications, and still with no prospect of success, he asked himself if there were not another way, and remembered something that happened to him as a child seated beneath a rose-apple tree. The impact and revelatory significance of the recollection are conveyed by the use of the verb abhijānāti, which, as we have seen, is so important in the

---

[*] Conze, op.cit., p.47.

[†] E.J. Thomas, *The Life of Buddha as Legend and History*, p.74. Aśvaghoṣa himself is thought to have belonged to one of the non-Mahāyāna sects into which Buddhism divided in the centuries following the Buddha's death. 'Though the Mahayanist teachings had been spreading for at least two or three centuries before his time, they find their first expression in his writings, in spite of the fact that he belonged to the Sarvastivada School.' P.V. Bapat et al., *2500 Years of Buddhism*, p.219.

Mūlapariyāya Sutta:

> I know it for a certainty: my Sākyan father was working in the fields
> and I was seated in the shade of a jambu tree, without desire or wrong
> in me, and I entered the first stage of meditation, which, generated in
> that state of mind, is thoughtful and earnest yet delightful. It was then
> that I wondered, Could this be the way to wisdom? And there came to
> me a consciousness equally convincing, that yes, this is the way.*

With such associations in the Sutta Piṭaka, it is not surprising that the
Buddha's birth was also believed to have taken place under a tree. This
is how it is described in the Introduction to the Jātaka tales.

> Queen Mahāmāyā bearing the Bodhisatta for ten months like oil in a
> bowl, when her time was come, desired to go to her relatives' house,
> and addressed king Suddhodana, 'I wish, O king, to go to Devadaha,
> the city of my family.' The king approved, and caused the road from
> Kapilavatthu to Devadaha to be made smooth and adorned with
> vessels filled with plantains, flags, and banners, and seating her in a
> golden palanquin borne by a thousand courtiers sent her with a great
> retinue. Between the two cities and belonging to the inhabitants of
> both is a pleasure grove of sāl-trees named the Lumbinī grove. At that
> time from the roots to the tips of the branches, it was one mass of
> flowers, and from within the branches and flowers hosts of bees of the
> five colours and various flocks of birds sported, singing sweetly.
> When the queen saw it, a desire to sport in the grove arose. The
> courtiers brought the queen and entered the grove. She went to the
> foot of a great sāl-tree, and desired to seize a branch. The branch like
> the tip of a supple reed bent down and came within reach of her hand.
> Stretching out her hand she seized the branch. Thereupon she was
> shaken with the throes of birth. So the multitude set up a curtain for
> her and retired. Holding the branch and even while standing she was
> delivered.†

Thus the life and death of the Buddha are inseparably associated with
trees, though they and the vegetal realm generally are a less rich source
of images than the animal kingdom.‡ The creeper represents

---

* *Mahāsaccaka Sutta,* MN.xxxvi.
† E.J. Thomas, op.cit. pp.32f.
‡ A notable exception to this statement is the lotus. See below page 59*n*.

obstructions in the path of virtue, especially, as mentioned above, the clinging dangers of sensuality. A palm tree utterly destroyed is a recurrent image for the destruction of passions. On the other hand, in the *Aṅguttara-Nikāya*, the immoral man is compared to a tree without branches or foliage, which comes not to full growth. The parts of a tree are used to represent the stages of the spiritual life, as noted earlier, the pith meaning ultimate freedom; this is the most elaborate arboreal image. The conventional metaphor of 'fruit' is used for arahantship. But perhaps the most striking usage involves the root (*mūla*), in the *Saṁyutta-Nikāya*, where the word *bhagavammūlakā* is found in a re-iterated phrase, *bhagavammūlakā no bhante dhammā*: 'For us, truths have as their root the Lord.'

The third great symbol of the Canon is found among the great elements. It is water. Not earth nor fire nor air is nearly so important. In the *Aggañña Sutta* we are told that when the universe enters its period of expansion there is but water and darkness, and only later, after a long, long time, does the earth appear upon the water. Thus, in a mythical sense, water is prior to earth, at least in becoming manifest to the primordial beings who populate space, lighting their darkness with their own inherent light. Its imaginal primacy is consistent with this.

The simplest usage of the image is an illustration of the First Noble Truth, the Truth of Sorrow. More than the waters of the sea, it is said, are the tears shed by beings in the long, long round of saṁsāra.

As the early Buddhists lived inland, and most of them probably never travelled to the far-off coasts, there are comparatively few references to seas and oceans. It is perhaps surprising that there are even so many. River and stream are more frequent images, especially the latter. The Pāli word is *sota* and on it are based the important terms *sotāpatti*, entering the stream of Dhamma, and *sotāpanna*, the convert who does so. The Western reader will be reminded of John baptizing in the Jordan and of Jesus entering the river. Unlike John's baptism, however, stream-entry for the Buddhist is not an outward act. Going into water means nothing in itself; in fact, the ritualistic attitude which sets store thereby is one of the fetters laid aside by the sotāpanna. In an earlier chapter an encounter was noted between the Buddha and a ritualist which gave the means of breaking those bonds:

Bathe in this wise, brahman: make peace among all beings,
Harming nought that draws breath, telling no lies,
Taking nothing not given, having faith, being generous.

As in the advice to the householder Sigāla, what we have here is the replacement of ritual with morality, the raising of life to a higher and freer level. All that is left of outwardness in stream-entry is the metaphor, whose significance is purely spiritual. Much of the Buddha's challenge to his time is to be found in his attitude to ritualism, which was so dominant a feature of Indian society, involving not only obvious cruelty but a neurotic element as well. Ritual can be a form of compulsive behaviour, no more healthy when performed under religious motivation than any other.

The Canon's best-known passage dealing with water is probably the famous simile of the raft, in the *Majjhima-Nikāya* (MN.xxii). Here a man comes upon a wide stretch of water which he wishes to cross to escape the dangers threatening him on the near side and to reach the other side, where he will find safety. So he makes a raft and crosses over. When he reaches the other side he leaves the raft behind. He does not carry it with him: even good and useful things must be abandoned when they have served their purpose. Commentators on this parable give most of their attention to the raft, but it is not without interest that when the wayfarer has reached the other shore he does not vanish or pass away or sit beneath a tree waiting for death: he walks on.

The image of water receives its most elaborate treatment, probably the most elaborate of any image, in the *Sāmaññaphala Sutta* (DN.ii). The title means 'The Fruits of Recluseship', and the discourse, touched upon earlier, is said to have been delivered by the Buddha to the parricidal King Ajātasattu of Magadha. It was the night of the full moon at the end of the rainy season, called the Night of Komudī, the white water lily, which was supposed to open then; so beautiful a night that Ajātasattu uttered a little paean in its praise:

How pleasant, soothing and auspicious
Is this moonlit night, my friends!

His delight would be complete if he could visit some wise man who would put his mind at ease. Six famous names are mentioned, but the king remains silent after each one, signifying that he has no wish to meet that particular recluse. Finally his physician Jīvaka suggests that he visit the Buddha, who happens to be staying in Jīvaka's own mango grove with a large following of monks, 1,250 in all. Ajātasattu agrees. Then the state elephant and 500 others are got ready, and the king and 500 of his women ride to the grove accompanied by torch-bearing attendants. But as they approach Ajātasattu is stricken with fear. He wonders if his physician is leading him into a trap. If there are so many monks about how can there be such silence? – not a sound of any description from supposedly so large a gathering. Jīvaka has to reassure him that this is not an ambush in waiting but truly a meeting of peaceful men. Then they come upon a lighted pavilion and in it are seated the Buddha and his bhikkhus, silent and calm as the waters of a lake. Ajātasattu is quite overcome and exclaims, 'I wish my beloved son might know such calm.'

Then he bows to the Buddha and salutes the bhikkhus, stretching forth his joined hands, and sits down and asks the Buddha about the benefits in this world of the reclusive life. He receives a very full reply. Starting from the honour a king will pay even to one of his own slaves who enters on the holy life, the Buddha discourses on all the stages of spirituality. At first the similes chosen in illustration have liberation as their theme – liberation from debt, illness, slavery. Then the theme changes, and picks up the suggestions found earlier – the Night of the Water Lily, the likening of the assembly to a clear lake. The exemplary recluse by now is 'estranged from lusts, aloof from evil dispositions' and enters the first jhāna, and his very body is filled with joy. A bath-house scene is evoked to suggest the sensation:

> *Just, O king, as a skilful bathman or his apprentice will scatter*
> *perfumed soap powder in a metal basin, and then besprinkling it with*
> *water, drop by drop, will so knead it together that the ball of lather,*
> *taking up the unctuous moisture, is drenched with it, pervaded by it,*
> *permeated by it within and without, and there is no !eakage possible.*

So is the state of the recluse at this stage. When he enters and abides in the second jhāna his joy is even greater.

> *Just, O king, as if there were a deep pool, with water welling up into*
> *it from a spring beneath, and with no inlet from the east or west, from*
> *the north or south, and the god should not from time to time send*
> *down showers of rain upon it. Still the current of cool waters rising*
> *up from that spring would pervade, fill, permeate, and suffuse the*

*pool with cool waters, and there would be no part or portion of the
pool unsuffused therewith.*

Of the serenity of the third jhāna the Buddha says:

*Just, O king, as when in a lotus tank the several lotus flowers, red or
white or blue, born in the water, grown up in the water, not rising up
above the surface of the water, drawing up nourishment from the
depths of the water, are so pervaded, drenched, permeated, and
suffused from their very tips down to their roots with the cool
moisture thereof, that there is no spot in the whole plant, whether of
the red lotus, or of the white, or of the blue, not suffused therewith.*

In the fourth jhāna it is

*as if a man were sitting so wrapt from head to foot in a clean white
robe, that there were no spot in his whole frame not in contact with
the clean white robe – just so, O king, does the Bhikshu sit there, so
suffusing even his body with that sense of purification, of
translucence, of heart, that there is no spot in his whole frame not
suffused therewith.*

The white robe was put on after bathing. It seems that we are to think
of someone emerging from a stream in which he has been immersed
totally.

An interval is now described, in which certain discoveries are made
by the recluse, before the theme of water is resumed. The striver has
finally won to knowledge of the Four Noble Truths and to freedom

---

* The importance of the lotus as an image goes right back to the origins of Buddhism.
When the Buddha had gained Enlightenment he is said to have doubted whether the
Dhamma would be comprehensible to a world dominated by sensuality, whereupon the
great god Brahmā Sahampati comes and urges him to teach. Then the Buddha surveys
the world with his new insight and sees beings at different stages of development, some
of whom will be disposed to listen. They are compared to various coloured lotuses at
different stages of growth, some of which rise out of the water. (See 'Discourse on the
Noble Quest' *Ariyapariyesana Sutta*, MN.xxvi.) Thus the lotus not only represents serenity,
as in the quotation above, but also spiritual growth as it emerges from its natural element
and opens in the light and air. In the Mahāyāna it gives its name to one of the most famous
scriptures, the *Saddharma Puṇḍarīka*, the 'Lotus of the True Law', especially important in
Japanese Buddhism in both ancient and modern times. In the Pāli Canon we are
impressed with the sheer delight that lotus pools gave – to the sage who admired their
colours and to the traveller who drank their waters and plunged into them to refresh his
limbs.

from rebirth. The realization of the final good is given in perhaps the most beautiful of all images in the Canon.

> *Just, O king, as if in a mountain fastness there were a pool of water, clear, translucent, and serene; and a man, standing on the bank, and with eyes to see, should perceive the oysters and the shells, the gravel and the pebbles and the shoals of fish, as they move about or lie within it: he would know: 'This pool is clear, transparent, and serene, and there within it are the oysters and the shells and the sand and gravel, and the shoals of fish are moving about or lying still.'*
>
> *This, O king, is an immediate fruit of the life of a recluse, visible in this world, and higher and sweeter than the last. And there is no fruit of the life of a recluse, visible in this world, that is higher and sweeter than this.*[*]

This may well be called the triumph of imagery in the Pāli Canon, for it conveys something of the nature of nibbāna which more prosaic statements never do. Its significance lies in the suggestion of life, both in the 'man standing on the bank and with eyes to see' and in the scene before him. The mountain pool is not dead or empty. It is not artificial. It is a natural formation with living beings in it. The man notes their existence and does not interfere.

When the poetic qualities of the Sutta Piṭaka are discovered, the old literature comes alive in a new way. As said earlier, some of the conventions of Indian literature are strange to us, as the likening of the Buddha to bull and lion and tiger. Even stranger is it to find someone likening the Buddha's destruction of an opponent's argument to the smashing of a crab by children: it is his way of giving praise and he sees nothing amiss in saying it to the Buddha's face. The Buddha does not thank him for the comparison. Nowhere else in the suttas is anything like this insensitivity displayed, all the worse as the opponent was a Jain, and thus a collaborator with Buddhism in the propagation of ahiṁsā. In the main, however, more familiar conventions are observed conformable with the spirit of the best poetry, which does not find incompatibility in representing an invisible realm by means of the visible. Furthermore, the use of images for meditational states suggests that when the recluse had 'done what was to be done' he did not

---

[*] Rhys Davids' translation of the *Sāmaññaphala Sutta* (DN.ii), *Dialogues of the Buddha*, part I.

withdraw into anything that might be denoted by the word 'apathy' as now used, but remained on appreciative terms with the visible world. This is obviously important as an indicator of the Buddhist attitude, for if the highest value of the system can be represented positively in terms derived from the world, it may be claimed that the world as a whole is of value in the system. And that series of images is supported by perhaps the most telling single image in the Canon, when the Buddha says 'As the sea has but one savour, that of salt, so the Dhamma has but one savour, that of freedom.' (AN.IV.201)

One feels obliged to labour this point because one finds it so often doubted and even denied by people who should know better. The philosopher Max Scheler expressed the common misconception as follows:

> Man is the kind of being who, by means of the spirit, can take an ascetic attitude toward life. He can suppress and repress his own vital drives and deny them the nourishment of perceptual images and representations. Compared with the animal that always says 'Yes,' to reality, even when it avoids it and flees from it, man is the being who can say 'No,' the 'ascetic of life', the protestant par excellence, against mere reality. This has nothing to do with any question of value or Weltanschauung. It does not matter whether we follow Buddha and say that this ascent of the spirit into the unreal sphere of essence is the ultimate goal and good of man because reality is inherently evil (omne ens est malum) or whether, as I believe, we must try to return from the sphere of essences to the reality of the world in order to improve it....*

It is not at all satisfactory to equate *malum* with dukkha, which is the idea in question here. The Buddha did not say: Two things I teach, evil and the end of evil. *Malum* lacks the inseparable note of sorrow, the *lacrimae rerum*, and the inseparable note of hope in the basic Buddhist statement, in which knowledge of sorrow is the beginning of wisdom. As for returning from the unreal sphere of essences to the reality of the world in order to improve it, the Buddha spent the forty-odd years of his life after the Enlightenment attempting to do precisely that, and to some effect, as history shows, for the Dhamma has brought not only spirituality but culture and refinement, reform and peace and

---

* *Man's Place in Nature*, pp.54f.

happiness to large portions of the world for long periods. Some of the societies it shaped have had to endure the impact of colonialism and communism and the ravages of modern war, but have come through with something of their Buddhist quality surviving. Now they face another enemy of Western origin, consumerism, which is only rāga, dosa, and moha in the guise of acquisitiveness and exploitation, driven by the power of advertising. It is not the only challenge the Dhamma faces, but it is the one which will put its relations with the natural world to the greatest test. At the same time it will give the greatest opportunity to show what an enlightened attitude may effect. The imagery of the Discourses – detailed, vivid, full of warmth and friendliness towards the world and nature – enables us to get some sense of this attitude on the imaginative level.

5

ENLIGHTENMENT AND WILDERNESS

CITY AND FOREST have each an important place in the biography of Gotama the Buddha and in the history of the religion he founded. The contrast between them gives rise to one of the most poetic passages in the early literature. It is found in a discourse allocated to Sāvatthī, the capital city of Kosala, north of the Ganges. The Buddha recalls the time before Enlightenment when he was still baffled by the mystery of existence, the seemingly endless round of birth and ageing and dying and returning. Then he found the method of the *paṭiccasamuppāda*, Dependent Origination: On what do ageing and dying depend? On birth. On what does birth depend? On bhava, the life-force; which depends ultimately on the interactions of transconsciousness and individuality (*viññāṇa, nāmarūpa*). 'The origin! The origin!' he exclaimed to himself, as knowledge, wisdom, and light flooded his mind, and he knew that if this interaction were ended the dependent sequence would not develop, and suffering would cease. So fundamental has this doctrine seemed that it has been equated with the Dhamma itself: Whosoever understands Dependent Origination understands the Truth. Its discovery was celebrated in a great image. It was, he said, as though a man going through the wilderness came upon a path, ancient but still straight, which had been followed by men of olden times; and following it himself he came upon an ancient city, once a royal seat, where those men of old had dwelt; a delightful resort with parks and groves and lakes and walls around. The man goes and tells the ruler of the land or his chief minister what he has found and begs him to restore the place. This is duly done, and the city becomes thriving, successful, and populous. 'Even so', says the Buddha, 'did I find a straight and ancient path, followed by the fully enlightened ones of old: the Noble Eightfold Path of right views, aims, speech, actions, livelihood, effort, mindfulness, and contemplation. Following this path I have come to know the truth of ageing and dying, how they originate, how they cease, and the way to their ceasing; and so with birth and the other factors of Dependent Origination, back to individuality and transconsciousness, and beyond these to the activities (*sankhārā*) on which their existence depends; and I have come to know the truth of these also, how they originate, how they cease and the way to their ceasing. Having come to know all this in truth, I have taught it to the monks and nuns, to the lay disciples, male and female: it is the holy life, thriving and successful, spreading to the masses, made known to all mankind.'[*]

What is of most interest to the present discussion is not so much the doctrinal matter as the balance or emphasis of the image. A man going through forest and jungle finds a path, overgrown but yet unerring, to a lost city, whose former beauty is still discernible; through his efforts the city is restored, and prospers. This appears to place the Buddha firmly on the side of 'culture' as against 'nature', and there is other evidence in the Canon to support the apparent preference. What has been called the Buddha's urbanity is well exemplified by the story of the city saved from the jungle. It has been noted

> ... that the setting of his life, from the first to the last days, was predominantly urban. It was a life spent in great centres where people came together to trade and to deliberate, to study and to practise their special crafts and industries, to discuss and to be entertained, to seek justice, to make money, or to find the truth. The appeal of his doctrines was primarily to men of an urban background. Among the things which, tradition suggests, might be said in praise of him was that he abstained from 'village ways' (gāmadhamma), a term which could also be translated 'vile conduct'. T.W. Rhys Davids suggests that the phrase means 'the practice of country folk ... the opposite of pori, urbane'. Later in the same passage it is said, in fact, that the words of the Buddha are 'pleasant to the ear, reaching to the heart, urbane (pori)'.[†]

[*] Paraphrase of SN.XII.65.
[†] Ling, *The Buddha*, pp.128f.

Warder is in agreement with this view. He notes how the Buddha and other samaṇas wandered from place to place 'discussing the problems of life with kings, ministers, soldiers, merchants, artisans and people of various professions, and unspecified "householders"'; similarly, how 'they were constantly in touch with the ordinary peasants or farmers, begging food from them, holding private conversations and giving public lectures'. He then observes: 'It is more remarkable, perhaps, to notice that the Buddha is recorded to have spent much of his time in the cities, or at least on their outskirts. His activities and organisation appear to have centred on the capitals of Magadha, Vṛji, Kośala and other countries, not on forest or mountain retreats.'*

This, however, leaves unexamined the Buddha's associations with the world outside the centres of human settlement, and an incomplete and unbalanced picture of his life is created as a result. There is a great deal of material in the early literature with which to correct it. Much of this material is of interest in its own right and as an index of attitudes to the natural world; some of it affords glimpses into deep levels of the Buddhist mind.

There are few descriptions of external nature in the Sutta Piṭaka. So it is in nearly all ancient literature, and indeed in most modern Western literature before the romantic revival. It is perhaps less surprising that there are few than that there are any at all. One such description occurs in another discourse dealing with the Enlightenment, and is of additional interest here because it also features a town and a wild place, though this time they are actual and not symbolic. In this discourse, 'On the Noble Quest' (*Ariyapariyesana Sutta*, MN.xxvi), the setting is once again the Kosalan city of Sāvatthī. While the Buddha is going his round, alms-bowl in hand, some monks approach his attendant, Ānanda, saying it is a long time since they have heard a talk on Dhamma from the Lord. Ānanda says they should go to the ashram of the brahman Rammaka, where the Buddha will likely visit them. Later in the day the Buddha and Ānanda go and bathe, then Ānanda suggests the Buddha visit the monks out of compassion for them, and he commends Rammaka's ashram as being a place of delight and beauty (*ramaṇīya, pāsādika*), knowing, it would seem, that this will weigh with the Buddha.

* A.K. Warder, *Indian Buddhism*, p.157.

The discourse delivered that evening contains much autobiographical material. Motivation for the quest is given in terms different from those of the preceding account, and the tone is one of disillusionment with all the world has to offer. If in the working out of the paṭiccasamuppāda one is reminded of Rilke's poem about the Buddha thinking 'thoughts before which our thinking shies away', here the stress is not on intellect but on feeling. 'Why do I, subject as I am to birth and ageing, to decline and death, to sorrow and passion, seek things that are themselves subject thereto? Should I not seek the unborn, the ageless, the undeclining, the deathless, untouched by sorrow and passion – nibbāna?' The Buddha's reminiscences to the monks of Sāvatthī suggest the most profound spiritual distress at the time of his going forth; and a facing up to feelings which might have destroyed so sensitive a nature. Presently he leaves home and sets out on the Noble Quest, a young man in the prime of life, cutting off his black hair and beard, and donning a yellow robe amid the lamentations of his mother and father. (There is nothing in this or the other Enlightenment narratives about Yasodharā and Rāhula, the wife and son made familiar to the West in *The Light of Asia.**) The young wanderer went to a great teacher, Āḷāra Kālāma, and became his disciple. Having mastered Āḷāra's teachings in short order, he decided not to stay with him as joint teacher of his group, and went on to a more advanced teacher, Uddaka Rāmaputta. The first teacher had taken the Bodhisatta to the sphere of nothingness, the second took him to the sphere of neither ideation-nor-non-ideation, but could go no further, could not, any more than Āḷāra, 'open the door of the deathless'. Once more the young man was on his own.

> So in the course of time, monks, still seeking the ultimate good,
> looking for the unsurpassable path to peace, I made my way through
> Magadha and came to the camp town of Uruvela. There I saw a
> delightful (ramaṇīya) stretch of ground and a beautiful (pāsādika)
> area of jungle and a clear flowing river with delightful banks and
> there were villages for support all around. It seemed just the right
> spot for one determined to make the supreme effort.

We cannot say that these are the Buddha's very own words. With their ramaṇīyas and pāsādikas they echo the description of the ashram earlier in the sutta, and this can hardly be put down to mere chance.

---

* See Thomas, op.cit., chapters 4 and 5, for an interesting discussion of this question.

But the passage has a freshness and clarity which goes well beyond stylistic niceties. Rarely in ancient literature is such a sense of place conveyed, such a sense of discovery. In contrast to the simile of the city in the jungle, here all the praise is bestowed on natural things – the stretch of ground, the Nerañjarā in springtime with its flowering banks, and the wild patch of woodland within walking distance of village and town. The passage beautifully anticipates the realization of nibbāna in the sutta, and reminds us that, whatever his later associations with town and city, the Buddha did not choose Uruvela itself but the country outside in which to make the final effort.

The third version of the Enlightenment is found in the 'Discourse on Fear and Dread' (*Bhayabherava Sutta*, MN.iv). There the contrast is between the wilderness and certain shrines, which latter are the symbols of culture; there is no mention of a city, real or symbolic, in the sutta. The atmosphere, too, is very different from the sunny openness of the Noble Quest. A brahman has been saying how hard it is to delight in the solitude of wild places, which can prove too much for a monk who has not mastered concentration. The Buddha agrees, but he also recalls how, before the Enlightenment, he benefited from living in the wilderness. It strengthened his self-assurance. Others might experience fear and dread, but this, he says, arises from their lack of loving-kindness and from something being amiss with their lives. It is their own nature and not that of the wild places that is to blame for the feelings that overcome them and for their inability to cope with them. Fortified then by the life he had led in the wilderness, the Bodhisatta began to move back towards civilization, and on the way he subjected himself to what might be called 'the Test of the Shrines', as he tells Jāṇussoṇi the brahman. This in brief is what he says:

'I had the idea of testing myself for fear and dread by staying at various shrines noted for their disturbing atmosphere. They were situated in woodland and parkland or at individual trees and I went to them on the nights appointed for the cult according to the phases of the moon. There in the darkness or in the moon-cast shadows I might hear some animal approaching or a bird might break off a twig or the wind might just rustle some fallen leaves, and I would think, Is this it coming now, the fear and dread? But after some time I thought, What am I doing here, wanting this to happen? And if it does happen, why should I not drive out any fear and dread? So, brahman, if those feelings arose in me as I was pacing up and down, or standing, or sitting, or lying down, I did not change from whichever of those activities I might be doing, but I faced that fear and dread just as it found me and drove it out.'

A number of these shrines are mentioned in the Sutta Piṭaka. Many were associated with the city of Vesālī, north of modern Patna. Although it was a place visited often by the Buddha, the Canon does not give enough information to let us know what the principal objects of worship were. But we may safely assume that the Licchavīs, whose capital Vesālī was, held beliefs no different from those obtaining in other parts of northern India, where the Vedic religion was still in full vigour.*

This may provide some explanation of the feelings of horror and distress aroused by the shrines: that not only were they in some way felt to be 'haunted', but that they may also have been places where blood-sacrifice was performed when the Buddha was a young man, and thus repugnant to his moral nature and requiring all the more resolution when he determined to brave their atmosphere. What is certain is that his reaction to these 'numinous' places was not one of 'holy dread' or self-surrender or submission, but of analysis and resistance, and final expulsion of what he considered to be an unwholesome state of mind. At the end of his life he could speak of them with affection; which indicates that his teaching and presence had purged them of cruelty and bloodiness.

From the conquest of fear and dread, the Bodhisatta goes on to achieve his aim. The atmosphere, night-set and oppressive up to now, changes as

ignorance was destroyed and knowledge arose,
darkness was dispelled and light arose.

The sutta ends with the Buddha telling the brahman that he still frequents remote places in the wild. 'You may think', he remarks, 'that I do so because I have not got rid of the roots of evil, rāga, dosa, and moha. Not so. My reasons are that I am happy living in the wilderness and that I have compassion for the lowly folk who are to be met there.'

---

* See B.C. Law, *Some Kśatriya Tribes of Ancient India*, p.65.

These three narratives, each with its special emphasis, fill out our picture of the Enlightenment. Biographically, the sutta on the Noble Quest has priority; it reveals something of Gotama's motivation and describes his going forth in plain, believable words; from it also we learn of his spiritual progress under his teachers and of his decision finally to go on alone. The town of Uruvela is simply mentioned; its interest is geographical; and after the Enlightenment it is not there the Buddha goes but to the deer-park of Isipatana, at Benares, where 'the Wheel of the Law was turned'.

In the narrative of the Lost City the emphasis is on the importance of the Noble Eightfold Path and of the Doctrine of Dependent Origination. At once philosophical, religious, and poetic, it conveys the complex intellectual tone of early Buddhism, its insistence on morality, and on the consequential nature of things, together with imaginative vision.

The third narrative, the 'Discourse on Fear and Dread', has no mention of towns, or of parents and teachers, and places all emphasis on the wilderness. The dialogue with the forest-repelled brahman brings out once again an idea that is central to the Buddhist view. The wilderness is acknowledged to be the sort of environment in which fear and dread arise, but the origins of these are not located in the place but in oneself, deficient in purity of body, speech, and mind, in calmness, modesty, and charity – 'not extolling myself, not disparaging others' – in energy, mindfulness, and concentration; or tainted with covetousness, sloth, doubt, ambition – 'striving after gains, honour, fame'. The Buddha agrees with Jānussoṇi the brahman, as said above, that dwelling in the wilderness is not easy, but his explanation is directed not at the outer world but inward to the heart of man, which projects its own wrong states upon the objects of its attention. In this instance the object is the wilderness, and impurity of heart reflects back from it as fear and dread. This sutta offers a correspondence, in terms of feeling, with the intellectual preoccupation of the *Mūlapariyāya Sutta*. The moral is similar: a great deal of basic work must be done by the individual upon himself not only before he can truly understand the world, as in the 'Root Discourse', but before he can experience it truly. Once he leaves his familiar existence and enters upon the homeless life, he may find himself a prey to all sorts of disturbing sensations. Unless he makes the discovery that it is his own corrupt heart which causes these he will go ever further astray, and bring ever more suffering upon himself and upon the world in which he locates his fears, and from which he may try to banish what he conceives to be the causes of them, perhaps using violence and destructiveness to do so, as fear so readily turns into fury. The Buddha describes himself as one of those who with friendly feelings frequent remote places in forest and wilderness. More pointedly he says *mettacitto 'ham asmi:* I am a man of loving-kindness.

For all that, however, it is not said that the Buddha was always free of fear and dread. On the contrary, he says that through this sojourn in the forest his confidence was strengthened, and he was thereby emboldened to brave the 'hair-raising' (*salomahaṁsa*) atmosphere of the shrines, those outposts of culture set up in groves and glades by timorous people. What this narrative establishes is that the conquest of fear is essential to the achievement of wisdom, and that the first step in the conquest of fear is reconciliation with the natural world by means of a loving heart. After that the horrors of the man-made world may be approached with confidence and converted to goodness, harmlessness, and delight.

It is notable that the 'Discourse on Fear and Dread' makes no reference to the teachers named in the 'Noble Quest'. It is as if the intention were to put aside as irrelevant the human influences which contributed to the Buddha's progress, concentrating exclusively on the non-human milieu. It might be something of an anachronism to speak of the influence of the wilderness – 'one impulse from a vernal wood' – but in the 'Fear and Dread' there is a direct encounter, in literature perhaps the first of all such encounters, between man and the wild, and its effect on the man is acknowledged by him. The 'impulse', as far as it can be discerned, was the Bodhisatta's own: the decision to dwell alone in the jungle, the spiritual striving while there, the testing of character which accompanied it. Without the wilderness, it seems reasonable to say, his development would have been incomplete, and would have been in some way inadequate to his mission among men. The import of this discourse, then, is that the wilderness has a fundamental value in itself, quite apart from the Āḷāras and Uddakas who may be met with there; that it is an essential element in the life of the Buddha; and that, with every concession to urbanity, the roots, if one may so put it, of the new life he taught, are to be found in the wilderness and not in the towns, in nature rather than in culture.

In wishing to give the wilderness its due, however, it would be wrong to suggest that this displaces the idea of the urbane Gotama and replaces it with a forest-dwelling recluse. It is true that he was wont to revisit the jungle, for his own pleasure and to meet those who for whatever reason frequented it; but his ministry, as Warder and the other authorities have said, was chiefly carried on in the towns. In thinking of the Buddha, town and wilderness must each be considered if we are to do justice to his career, and if his importance for the present day is to be more fully appreciated. Part of his importance I believe to reside in his symbolic power as reconciler of civilization and nature. One approach to the question of reconciliation is through the notion of complementary contrast.

It will be recalled that in the second Enlightenment story, the town of Uruvela was described simply in terms of function: it is called a *senānigāma*, an army town; we are not told anything else about the place. The land around is described vividly and in terms of pleasure. The word 'ramanīya' is twice used, once of the spot in general and once of the riverside: they are both said to be delightful. The repetition arrests the reader's attention a moment. Pāli is a rich language, with no shortage of words to convey pleasure. Why use 'ramanīya' twice in such close proximity?

'Ramanīya' becomes even more arresting in the story of the Buddha's last days (DN.xvi), where its repetition is so insistent that no doubt can remain as to its being a stylistic device, albeit possibly one based on the Buddha's own usage. He is reported as praising the city of Vesālī and its shrines by means of this word and as recalling other places that pleased him, and all of them are called ramanīya. Some of them are wild and some urban and 'ramanīya' unites them all, conferring its favour equally on the works of man and the products of nature. It goes beyond the contrast found in the other suttas, one with its delightful lost city in the jungle, the other with its delightful country around a town, and brings everything together in a unity of delight, as perhaps we may, without impropriety, suppose them to have been in the Buddha's mind. The one thing not praised in all of this is the functionality of Uruvela the army town.

If these discourses have a meaning for the present time it is surely to be found in this vivid word 'ramanīya' and in some principle of delight which would bring nature and culture together in a fruitful union and not in conflict any more. The implication of the suttas, in my reading of them, is that human works and humanized places come nearest the Buddhist ideal when they give delight as a wild place can, though not of course the same delight. It will be recalled that the lost ideal city is described as ramaṇīya, and has parks and groves and lakes within its walls – a place, that is, drawing inspiration from the jungle all around, and, though distinct, not cut off from it. It was not a fortress under siege from a non-human enemy which must either be destroyed or subjected to the notion of utility and function, and thus made empty of delight. On restoration it would remain open to the delight-giving quality of the wild and embody it in its own life. The unity of delight mentioned above would find expression in a harmony of man and the natural world, as free as possible from exploitation and acquisitiveness, that is, from a mentality, an outlook, and a standard based on rāga, dosa, and moha.

But yet, having said this, the spectre of adhamma remains, the grim words spoken of the animal world, in which 'there is found no living by the dhamma, no living at peace, no doing good or meritorious deeds; they are caught up in a cycle of mutual destruction and devouring and preying on the weak.'

A vivid picture of what used to be called 'the Law of the Jungle'; a reminder that the Noble Truth of Dukkha holds not only in human affairs but throughout the living world – in the wilderness, which is also, however, said to be ramaṇīya. Two opposing concepts seem here to meet head-on.

As said before, it is a commonplace of Western writing about Indians, both modern and ancient, that they find no trouble in holding contradictory ideas. It would probably be as true to say that Westerners find great difficulty in handling disparate ideas and are all too prone to describe difference as contradiction and hence impossible of reconciliation. But it is not always a question of reconciliation. That can be an occasion of mere cosmetic intellectualism. A greater difficulty, a more real challenge, may lie in *not* reconciling contradictions but in being able to live with them. Again it is also a commonplace to describe Buddhism as practical; whether classed as a religion or as a philosophy this term is commonly invoked to qualify it. If the word means anything it should indicate that Buddhism is notable for its helpfulness to those who are endeavouring to uphold and to realize its ideals: that it is not only a set of precepts but a provider of aids towards keeping them; a consistent system of thought which in addition is able to deal with seeming inconsistencies. Other systems may invoke the theological virtue of faith. This is not available to Buddhism, the *saddha* of which is a different thing, though the word most commonly used to translate it is 'faith'. Nor is submission to an inscrutable Divine Will one of its requirements or ideals: *en sua voluntade è nostra pace* – such a sentiment is not found in the Pāli Canon, not even on the lips of the brahmans, it is probably true to say.

How does Buddhism deal with an intellectually insoluble clash of ideas? That ideas should come to such a pass is only to be expected, given the Buddhist estimate of intellect, its limitations, and its place in the life of man. It is pertinent to recall here the words of Giuseppe Tucci quoted earlier.

> *In India the intellect has never prevailed to the extent of obtaining mastery over the faculties of the soul, of separating itself therefrom and thus of provoking that dangerous scission between the intellect and the psyche which is the cause of the distress from which the Western world suffers. The West, indeed, as though to designate its present inclinations, has coined a new word, unwonted in the history of human thought, the word 'intellectual' – as though it were possible to have a type of man reduced to pure intellect.*

Tucci's terminology with its 'soul' and 'psyche' may not be immediately in accord with Buddhism, but this does not detract from the point and relevance of his words. In the Buddhist model of man the intellect is most readily accommodated to the functions of the saññākkhaṇdha. But the thrust of the khandha teaching is the falsity of identifying the person with any one faculty, even the highest, if that be intellect. A Buddhist cannot, therefore, *define* himself as an 'intellectual' any more than he can define himself simply in terms of the feelings or the body.

What this means in practice is that the Buddhist cannot look to any one of the khandas alone for the solution of life's problems. If intellect alone could provide answers it would certainly be the greatest faculty. But the 'Root Discourse' leaves no doubt that from the Buddhist viewpoint intellectual operations, even the highest, are likely to be influenced by unacknowledged factors. Even when touched by a higher mode of knowledge the intellect is not in itself an adequate guide without the practice of morality. But neither are the feelings an adequate guide. If fanaticism is unbalanced, so is sentimentality in its less offensive way. The Dhamma deals with man in his entirety and it is man in his entirety and not merely as feelings or intellect that solutions are to be found. The body too has a part to play in any quest for truth based on an Indian prescription. All the khandhas, with their activities and the consequences of these, are inseparable from the idea of the whole person. Buddhism is the Doctrine of the Middle Way. Ancient India produced extreme attitudes to life in the teachings and in the persons of its great sages; dire asceticism on the one hand and conscienceless indulgence on the other. The Buddha saw error in both. The Western tradition has produced extreme attitudes to intellect. At the end of the nineteenth century Irving Babbit noted them in these words:

> *The modern world is coming more and more to seek its salvation in*
> *the development of the reason and intelligence; and from this point of*
> *view Renan is consistent in exalting 'curiosity' above all other*
> *virtues. Christianity, on the other hand, may justly be suspected of*
> *having insufficiently recognized from the start the role of the intellect,*
> *and at times has inclined to show a special tenderness toward*
> *ignorance. Pascal was but true to the tradition of the Christian*
> *mystics when he branded the whole process of modern scientific*
> *inquiry as a form of concupiscence* libido sciendi, *the lust of*
> *knowing. When he felt the rise within him of the new power of reason*
> *which threatened the integrity of his medieval faith, he exclaimed in*
> *self-admonishment, 'You must use holy water and hear Masses, and*
> *that will lead you to believe naturally and will* make you stupid.'*

If self-stupefaction has no place in Buddhism, neither has the exaltation of curiosity to the highest function of mind. Curiosity may be supreme in the world of science, but that does not raise it 'above all other virtues' in a Buddhist perspective. The statement, attributed to Bertrand Russell, that 'what science cannot tell us, mankind cannot know' makes less than the highest sense from the viewpoint of a system directed towards freedom and 'the full perfection and grandeur of wisdom'.

If intellect is inseparable from the idea of the whole person, it is not then to intellect but to the whole person that Buddhism must look when ideas seem headed inevitably for conflict, the two ideas in question here being dukkha and delight. This means that the problem assumes an existential rather than an intellectual character in Buddhism. The question is not so much how can the ideas be reconciled, or how can one be

* *Representative Writings*, p.217.

shown as the more central or dominant of the two, but how is it possible to live with the conflict which they seem bound to generate in the mind of anyone who has to do justice to them both?

The first point to be noted in attempting to deal with this difficulty is that the Buddha dealt with it in living the life he is reported to have lived. And as he did not apparently see any necessity to give advice as to how it should be done, one is free to assume that the co-existence of the ideas of dukkha and delight came about and continued to be, without any direct specific effort on his part. This suggests two related things: first, that such conflict as the confrontation of disparate ideas may generate may be *only* intellectual; second, that the conflict can be, so to say, contained in the intellect without leading to a general psychological conflict; in other words, that the mind as a whole has resources which are not available to intellect alone; more specifically, that it has a tolerance of contrarieties which may come to be the despair of intellect, when intellect usurps or displaces the functions of the other faculties.

Another point to be noted is that Buddhist cultures, that is, those societies most deeply influenced by the Buddhist ethos, have found ways of living not oblivious to sorrow while expressive of joy. It would be inappropriate to undertake an historical relation here, but one can point to the artistic heritage of Buddhism in confirmation of the statement. Dukkha, often under the aspect of compassion, which may be represented by a soteric attitude or a healing gesture, is rarely absent from the work of Buddhist artists. Sometimes it may be conveyed impressionistically in the atmosphere of a landscape without any symbolical suggestion that one can discern. But in either case the effect is not only, or, it may be, not even predominantly, one of sadness, but of joy, and not a mere secular, aesthetic pleasure, stimulated by the formal qualities of the particular painting or statue or building. If, as is often the case, the artist was not only a gifted practitioner of his art, but also devoted to the discipline of the Dhamma, the effect may go far beyond this.

Without the Enlightenment there would be no Buddhism and thus no Buddhist art. Is it too much to find in the suttas devoted to the great event the seed of that wonderful flowering of religious creativity? I refer especially to the passage in the sutta on the Noble Quest, that small but vivid instance of response to landscape. The general context – the Bodhisatta's departure from home and grieving parents, his struggles and disappointments – leaves no doubt as to the dukkha of his existence. At the end all this is changed and he is the Buddha. The moment of transition is the arrival at Uruvela, with its 'delightful stretch of land', its grove and river. The description is placed between the failures and the triumph, but at the time of reading it one has only been made aware of the struggle and the failures. The delight transmitted by the passage arises primarily from the description, secondarily from anticipation. Because of the structure of the narrative one comes to the description in a condition of sympathetic sadness. The description in virtue of its own inherent qualities, apart from its indicating the setting of the Buddha's imminent victory, performs in a small but perfect way the functions of the best Buddhist art. It is founded upon dukkha but not dominated by it; it gives joy in its own right and points beyond itself to the end of sorrow.

In more general terms we may accordingly say, perhaps, that Buddhist art, society, and personality are alike expressions of dukkha and delight in balanced relation to one another, in harmonious and creative tension with one another, conducing toward a serene equipoise beyond the turbulence of intellect, the vagaries of feeling, and the frailty of the body.

6

THE UNKNOWN MYTH OF BUDDHISM

IF IN THE DESCRIPTION of the scene near the camp town of Uruvela we may see the beginnings of Buddhist art, so it may be claimed that in the *Aggañña Sutta* is to be seen the first great feat of the creative imagination in the literature. By this I mean the presentation of essential ideas in a form that brings them vividly to life and gives an insight into them not always found in the usual modes of presentation. This is all the more interesting in view of the ostensible subject of the sutta, for it is something of a commonplace of Buddhist studies that none of the great branches of the Dhamma has anything worth considering in the way of creation stories. The most eminent authorities are among the most emphatic. Edward J. Thomas wrote:

> The details of Buddhist cosmology need not detain us, as the fantastic structure appears to be merely based on the astronomical and geographical views of the time, but much of it was evidently elaborated and extended more or less independently by the Buddhists. The whole universe, corresponding to the egg of Brahmā, is divided into three regions, the kāmaloka, the world of sensuous feeling.... Above this is the rūpaloka, including the Brahma-heavens in sixteen stages, and ... the arūpaloka, the formless world.... But this is only one universe. There are other systems of these spherical universes, and in the spaces between them are special hells.*

---

* op.cit., p.207.

No one would guess from this sort of statement that the Pāli Canon had a myth of its own in the *Aggañña Sutta*; and Edward Conze, an equally authoritative scholar, added to the general misunderstanding. 'If Atheism is the denial of the existence of a God', he wrote,

> *it would be quite misleading to describe Buddhism as atheistic. On the other hand, Monotheism has never appealed to the Buddhist mind. There has never been any interest in the origin of the Universe – with only one exception. About* 1000AD *Buddhists in the North-West of India came into contact with the victorious forces of Islam. In their desire to be all things to all men, some Buddhists in that district rounded off their theology with the notion of an* Adibuddha, *a kind of omnipotent and omniscient primeval Buddha, who through his meditation originated the Universe. This notion was adopted by a few sects in Nepal and Tibet.*[*]

To be sure, there is nothing in Buddhism accorded the overwhelming authority of the Book of Genesis in the Judaeo-Christian tradition, nothing which has exercised such fascination over the mind and heart of the East as the story of Adam and Eve, the serpent, and the forbidden fruit has over the mind and heart of Christendom. Indeed there are texts which seem to give support to the general opinion that the early Buddhists had no interest in creation and fall. 'Incalculable', we read in one of the texts, 'is the starting-point in the career of beings blocked by ignorance, fettered by craving.' Then there is the famous so-called silence of the Buddha on certain questions, to which, he stated, dogmatic answers were not desirable. The first two groups of these *avyākatas* have to do with whether the world is or is not infinite and everlasting. The Buddha's position is that anyone who devotes his best energies to opinions on morally indifferent matters can hardly be aware of his real predicament.[†]

On the strength of these and of some other passages with a similar tone, the belief has arisen that Buddhism has nothing of interest to say about the beginning or the non-beginning of things. Yet there is little

---

[*] *Buddhism, Its Essence and Development*, pp.42f.

[†] As T.R.V. Murti writes, 'The *locus classicus* of this view is the *Cūḷamālunkya Sutta*.' There is found the famous simile of the wounded man who will not accept aid until he knows all about the arrow that is stuck in him and all about the person who shot it. In this and other dialogues Murti sees the birth of dialectic, 'long before anything approximating to it was formulated in the West'. (*The Central Philosophy of Buddhism*, pp.36ff.)

enough in these passages to warrant the belief. The Buddha is said to have used certain words in connection with the physical and temporal qualities of the universe but he would not have it that these are of ultimate importance in making sense of the world. Instead he tried to direct the attention of his hearers away from them to the decisiveness of man's moral nature in conditioning the world, that is, to the consequences of actions characterized by self-interest, ill-will, and delusion. This is the real burden even of the myth attributed to him in the *Aggañña*. In other words it may be said that the Buddha was asserting the independence of moral norms from religious myth and saying that the most diverse ideas were allowable provided they did not clash with moral living. This is not in any way to impugn Right View and its primacy in the Noble Eightfold Path. Right View means the acceptance of certain fundamental postulates; but it leaves immense latitude for morally neutral or harmless opinions and beliefs. Buddhism was the first great missionary religion. Its success was based on the ability to distinguish between what was and what was not essential among the teachings attributed to its founder. The cosmology of the *Aggañña Sutta*, related as it was to a particular social system and estimate of time, did not travel far outside of India, but its essential message did.

Something of this sort requires to be said prior to a discussion of the *Aggañña Sutta*, lest it should seem that some claim to dogmatic status is being put forward for its cosmology. The *Aggañña* has never enjoyed any such status; rather the opposite is true and if anything it has been neglected. Yet it is a precious heritage of the Buddhist world, a text worthy of the deepest study, and that not because of its cosmological but because of its moral content, and this would still be so even if its cosmology were demonstrated as correct in every detail. In fact it would be truer to describe the *Aggañña Sutta* as a moral rather than a creational myth. And if the form is exotic and fabulous, the morality is perfectly standard. Whoever gave it to the world was imbued with Buddhist principles to the marrow of his bones, and used mythic form as an expressive, potent means of conveying them.

Was this the Buddha himself? No one can say. There is no certainty that any statement in the Canon represents his words precisely, though we can be confident the essence of his teaching has been transmitted in the dogmatic formulas; there all the schools agree. Probably the most that can be claimed for any text is that it is in accord with the formulas. If this does not entitle it to be called *buddhavacana*, the Buddha's own words, it does confer the sanction of orthodoxy. Certainly on the basis of this argument, a high degree of orthodoxy may be accredited to the *Aggañña Sutta*; a number of essential ideas, elsewhere expressed in formulas, are to be discovered in it, only activated into narrative and so not immediately apparent.

In passing it might be useful to say a word here about dogma in Buddhism. It is often said that Buddhism is not a dogmatic religion. To be sure it has no theological dogmas. The Mahāyāna has wonderful elaborations of Buddhological ideas, the Trikāya being the best known. But this idea of the Three Bodies of the Buddha – the Body of Transformation, the Body of Bliss, and the Body of Reality – has not the essential and sometimes enforced status of Trinitarian dogma in Christianity. The Five Precepts might be called moral dogma, but they are free of the paradox of the Mosaic Code, which says 'Thou shalt not kill,' yet commands the killing of people who violate certain parts of the Code. The three Semitic religions, as a result of actions committed when they have had power, have brought the ideas of dogma and sanction into an almost inseparable conjunction. Buddhism, with its freedom from divinely inspired texts and its distrust of earthly (and indeed heavenly) power, does not compel morality either by present force or future threat. Karma is justice inherent in the nature of things and needs no authority to implement it. The first sīla does not only forbid cruelty to animals. Its scope is much wider than that. It also forbids the persecution of unbelievers and the burning of heretics, the stoning of adulterers and the mutilation of thieves.

The myth of the *Aggañña Sutta* begins with a description of happy beings, ancestors of man, moving through the darkness of space in the time between the contractive and expansive phases of the aeon; it ends with verses attributed to one of the sons of Brahmā. But neither Brahmā nor his sons have any part to play in the formation of the universe as narrated in the myth. Buddhist references to Brahmā, in fact, tend to be less than flattering. Much of the humour scattered throughout the Sutta Piṭaka is humour at Brahmā's expense. But these passages and others allow us to see something of the religious background against which Buddhism developed and they tell us a good deal about the attitude of the early Buddhists to the divinities worshipped by their contemporaries. One of the droller pieces of debunking is found in the *Kevaddha Sutta* (DN.xi) which tells the story of a monk who went to heaven and returned unsatisfied. He was troubled by a problem of the ultimate kind: Where do the great elements pass away leaving no trace behind? It seemed such an ultimate question that only an ultimate being could answer it. So, as Henry Clarke Warren's translation puts it, he 'worked himself up into such a state of ecstasy that the way leading to the world of the gods became clear to his ecstatic vision'. The monk goes to the devas at different levels of devahood, but none of them knows the answer. Finally he comes to the sphere of Brahmā and puts his question once more. The story goes on:

> And when he had thus spoken the gods of the retinue of Brahmā replied: 'We, brother, do not know that. But there is Brahmā, the Great Brahmā, the Supreme One, the Mighty One, the All-seeing One, the Ruler, the Lord of all, the Controller, the Creator, the Chief of all, appointing to each his place, the Ancient of days, the Father of all that are and are to be! He is more potent and more glorious than we. He will know it.'
>
> 'Where then is that Great Brahmā now?'
>
> 'We, brother, know not where Brahmā is, nor why Brahmā is, nor whence. But, brother, when the signs of his coming appear, when the light ariseth, and the glory shineth, then will He be manifest. For that is the portent of the manifestation of Brahmā when the light ariseth and the glory shineth.'
>
> And it was not long, Kevaddha, before that Great Brahmā became manifest. And that brother drew near to him, and said: 'Where, my friend, do the four great elements – earth, water, fire, and wind – cease, leaving no trace behind?'
>
> And when he had thus spoken that Great Brahmā said to him: 'I, brother, am the Great Brahmā, the Supreme, the Mighty, the All-seeing, the Ruler, the Lord of all, the Controller, the Creator, the Chief of all, appointing to each his place, the Ancient of days, the Father of all that are and are to be.'
>
> Then that brother answered Brahmā, and said: 'I did not ask you, friend, as to whether you were indeed all that you now say. But I ask you where the four great elements – earth, water, fire, and wind – cease, leaving no trace behind?'
>
> Then again, Kevaddha, Brahmā gave the same reply. And that brother, yet a third time, put to Brahmā his question as before.

*Then, Kevaddha, the Great Brahmā took that brother by the arm and
led him aside, and said:*

*'These gods, the retinue of Brahmā, hold me, brother, to be such that
there is nothing I cannot see, nothing I have not understood, nothing
I have not realised. Therefore I gave no answer in their presence. I do
not know, brother, where those four great elements – earth, water, fire,
and wind – cease, leaving no trace behind. Therefore you, brother,
have done wrong, have acted ill, in that, ignoring the Exalted One,
you have undertaken this long search, among others, for an answer to
this question. Go you now, return to the Exalted One, ask him the
question, and accept the answer according as he shall make reply.'**

The occasion of the *Aggañña Sutta* is the disquiet of two young brahmans, Vāseṭṭha and Bhāradvāja, on probation among the Buddhist
monks. Their decision to join the Order had not been well-received by
their fellow brahmans, who reviled them as betrayers of the highest
caste born of Brahmā's mouth, choosing to associate with the offspring
of Brahmā's feet. This means that in the eyes of the priestly caste the
Buddha and his followers are no better than the suddas, the lowest
caste. In the *Rig Veda*, which is the background to the *Aggañña Sutta*, as
to much else in the Canon, the Cosmic Man is sacrificed and from his
divided body the four castes arise: brahmans from his mouth, warriors
from his arms, the trading caste from his thighs, and the menials from
his feet. Thus brahmans are the dearest children of God, and the
decision to join a low-caste sect – a decision which many brahmans
made, including some of the early leaders of the new movement – is
one claimed to bring degradation on the caste-traitors. The Buddha
says that their attitude itself degrades their God and is a lie inasmuch
as they are born in the same way as everyone else; in other words they
are taking their myth literally and imposing it on others. All the castes,
he says, have good and bad members, people who uphold and people
who violate the principles of right living – a commonplace today, but
perhaps rather more than that in ancient India. It is not within the
castes, he says, but without that the highest type is to be found: among
the community of monks, drawn from all classes and transcending
them.

* Warren's translation, incorporated in Rhys Davids' version of the *Kevaddha Sutta*,
Dialogues of the Buddha, part III.

Follows the first mention of kingship, in the person of Pasenadi of Kosala, in whose domain the discourse is set. Kingship is one of the main themes of the discourse. The Buddha's people, the Sākyans, are subjects of King Pasenadi, yet he is said to do homage to the Sākyan Teacher. The king represents one principle, but recognizes that a higher principle is embodied in this member of the subject people. Thus the supreme status of the Dhamma is illustrated, at the same time as it is identified with the Tathāgata, who says:

Upon being asked 'Who are you?' let your reply be, 'We are samaṇas in the discipline of the Sākyan.' When faith in the Tathāgata is certain, radical, fixed, and firm, not to be subverted by recluse or brahman or deva or Māra or Brahmā or anyone in the world, then it is right to say, 'I am a true son of the Bhagavant, born of his mouth, the offspring and creation and heir of the Dhamma.' Why so? Because the Tathāgata may be described as the Body of the Dhamma, as the Body of Brahmā, as the being who is Dhamma and Brahmā.

The beginnings of the Mahāyāna are to be found in this passage, but that is outside the scope of this study. Suffice it to say that the Tathāgata is exalted to a glory beyond the human and that this is the note on which the myth of the *Aggañña Sutta* is introduced.

The introductory passage is cast in terms familiar to the Buddha's listeners, brought up on a cyclical theory of expansion and contraction. The universe is in the latter phase at the start of the narrative, turning in on itself after the passage of a long, long time, such as perhaps only the Indian mind, with its tremendous command of number, could then comprehend. Most beings by then have been reborn in the Realm of Radiance, the others having won to nibbāna or gone to less happy abodes. These Radiant Beings, the Ābhassaras, are described as made of mind, nourished on bliss, and emanating a light by which they move through space, glorious and beautiful. And so they live for a long time, but gradually they begin to decline from the Realm of Radiance. Although they are still described as mind-made beings, blissful, self-luminous, mobile, and beautiful, a change is also indicated. It seems to be a change of appearance precursive of human form, at least to the extent, as is said presently, of their having hands. But they were not yet sexually differentiated: 'there was neither female nor male; beings were accounted beings only.'

Meanwhile the contractive movement of the universe has come to an end, and it begins to unfold, but only as a watery mass in darkness, for there was neither sun nor moon, nor stars, nor years nor any other division of time.

Thus far three of the four great elements have been introduced, at least in proximate form: first fire, represented by the Radiants; then air, by the space through which they move; third, water, pouring through the darkness. Last of all the earth appears, though not in such a form that could as yet be called paṭhavī. Instead it is termed *rasapaṭhavī*, the essential, unmodified element in all its purity. By the light of their own forms the Radiant Beings see it extended on the waters, like the skin of rice boiled in milk when it is cooling. It had the colour of ghee or fine butter and was as sweet as honey.

As from the chaos of darkness and water the primordial earth emerges, so from the undiscriminated swarms of Radiants one is now distinguished. The mark of this being's distinction is a moral quality. *Satta lolajātika* is the designation: a restless, curious, greedy being. It is from this disposition that all consequences follow. This being initiates the wrong relations which have obtained between man and the world. 'What can this be?' it asks, approaching the pure earth, and without further ado puts a finger into it and tastes. The substance permeates the mental body of the inquisitive Radiant and craving – *taṇhā*, one of the key words in Buddhism – arises. Other beings then approach the pure earth and taste it, and they too are overcome with taṇhā. Soon they are gorging themselves on the honey-sweet primal substance, which has, under their attentions, begun to harden, so that instead of putting their hands into it, as at first, they now break it off in lumps. Meanwhile a change has taken place in the beings themselves: their self-luminance has begun to fade. With the fading of their self-luminance, the heavenly bodies appear and measured time is marked: 'moon and sun became visible, and stars and constellations, and night and day, and months and half-months, and seasons and years.'*

Herewith the first part of the narrative comes to an end: 'So far, at this point,' says the Buddha, 'the world had evolved.' But already the

---

* Since elsewhere in the Canon the sun and moon are called gods, it may be that here we have an implied theogony, i.e. that man in some way brings his gods into being. There is more obviously a chronogony, involving a measurable time which differs from the vast vague procession of the kalpas, the rhythm of saṁsāra.

decisive thing had happened: a wrong relationship with the world had been set afoot. The three roots of evil, never entirely destroyed in the Radiant Beings, had become active again. They have shown themselves to be greedy and heedless of the consequences of their actions. Next, some of them show ill-will to the least favoured of their kind.

As they continue to feed on the earth-substance, their bodies become ever solider and some appear to be more beautiful than others, and are filled with pride, thinking 'We are comelier than they.' This private voicing of ill-will has the consequence that the essential earth disappears. Then these beings, grief-stricken, gather to bewail its loss.

It was not a total loss, however. The disappearance suggests rather a great change than a vanishing. We read that out of the soil a plant resembling the mushroom in its growth appeared, with the same qualities of colour and taste as the essential earth had before. The beings eat and are nourished and their bodies grow solider than before and once again some believe themselves to be comelier than others and the old pride and ill-will are repeated. Then another change comes over the earth as the mushroom-like growths disappear, to be replaced by a plant whose mode of growing resembles that of a creeper; and this too has the selfsame qualities of the essential earth, that is, the colour of fine ghee or butter, and the taste of flawless honey. But the beings who eat of it grow denser still in body and again degrees of beauty are perceived and pride and ill-will are felt and again the environment is changed, and the creeper disappears. And the beings gather and weep for their loss once more.

Up to this point in the narrative the nature of the plants named has given rise to scholarly debate. But the next one is familiar: it is rice. It differs from its predecessors in another respect also, being the first plant not to have the colour and taste of the earth-essence. On its first appearance, however, by way of compensation it is free of husk and reproduces overnight wherever it has been gathered.

A new phase in human development now begins. Not only do the beings grow denser in substance as a result of eating the new food, with gradations of beauty as before, but sexual characteristics appear in some of them, and for the first time the terms women and men are used (in that order). Finding fascination in each other these engage in sexual activity (*methuna*). The neuters do not know what is going on and think they are mistreating each other. 'How could one being behave so foully to another?' they cry, and violently drive them away. Unwittingly they continue the attitude of the proud beings of earlier times, and contravene the First Precept with their violence, although the focus of their ill-will is now moral rather than aesthetic.

To their credit, however, they do not long persist in their animosity and after a few weeks they have recovered sufficiently to allow the men and women back among them. These are so absorbed in the pleasures of methuna that they build houses to enjoy themselves in privacy. This is acceptable and no more is said about sex. Their behaviour is called *asaddhamma* – 'not the very best thing they might be doing' – but the attitude to it is perfectly relaxed, as it has always been in Buddhist societies. Of far greater importance than sex in the story – and in a totally different category – are acquisitiveness and greed.

Before going on to consider the second part of the *Aggañña*, dealing not only with the formation of the caste-system but also foreshadowing the Buddhist Order, it may be useful at this juncture to review what has gone before.

It was noted that the evolution of the cosmos was conceived in terms of the four great elements and that the radiant precursors of man represented the light, shining in an otherwise unbroken darkness. These beings and the primal earth, however, are shown as quite separate in the beginning and their encounter is not predetermined. In this respect the *Aggañña Sutta* differs profoundly from the Book of Genesis. Precursive man is not passively placed in an already prepared environment whose previous fortunes are no concern of his. He is not summoned to life by a higher power which lays down the conditions of his fate. Instead, he finds himself contemplating an undifferentiated neutral and mutable primal substance in the light of his own intelligence. He is presented as the arbiter of its destiny from the very beginning, even as his successor is today. But at that time, for a while, he forbore to act, for there was an interval during which the mind-made precursors of the human race contemplated without interference the new world which had emerged from the waters. One is free to assume that all sorts of possibilities were present then, if only the right initiative had been taken. But this did not happen. Curiosity and greed, both contained in the word *lolajātika*, are the factors dominating the primordial relationship between these beings and their environment, an environment represented as sensitive and responsive not only to actions but to attitudes. However, the myth does not suggest that such a relationship is predetermined and that none other is possible. Some relationship would seem to be inevitable, for the very good reason that the four great elements are shared between the prehumans and the earth in their respective immediate environments: Radiant Beings in dark air, earth in the waters. Unless the four come together, there will be no humanized world and no material beings, only formless matter and immaterial forms. The antithetical positions are so nicely made out, one is tempted to take the myth as meaning that those beings and the earth are incomplete without each other. This may be so. But there is nothing in the myth to suggest that no other relationship could have developed and that greed, ill-will, and folly had to predominate.

The latter portion of the *Aggañña Sutta* has in recent years attracted the attention of Western scholars. Dealing as it does with property, order, kingship, and social divisions, its interest for anthropologists and sociologists is obvious. In addition it enunciates, perhaps for the first time in literature, the idea of the social contract, as well as that of the co-operative society, with acquisitiveness deemed a social, as throughout the rest of the Sutta Piṭaka it is deemed a personal, evil. This part of the myth, however, although mundane in comparison with what has gone before, is not without problems. The most notable of these is the statement, repeated, that the warrior caste, the khattiya, is the best of the social groups. It will be remembered that the burden of the sutta is the refutation of brahman pretensions to supremacy over the other castes. This being so, it seems at first glance a little anomalous to chasten the priests, only thereafter to exalt the warriors. Before attempting to deal with this, however, let us first see how the latter part of the discourse develops, following on the uneasy beginnings of family life.

Misconceived providence is the new motif. It arises out of the disposition of a certain person who is not overfond of exertion. Instead of making two journeys to fetch rice each day, he finds it less bothersome to fetch a double amount on one. He commends the practice to one of his fellows; the word is spread, and presently the people are gathering and storing for as many as eight days in advance. This labour-saving venture entails an unforeseen consequence, however, as the quality of the rice declines and it becomes less easy to handle. Whereas before it had neither powder nor husk, now it has both; before, it grew as it was gathered, now there are stubbly clumps where the reaper's hand has been at work.

Now once more the people come together to bemoan their lot. If they have learned nothing, they have forgotten nothing: they review all the stages of their decline from Radiant Beings aglow with bliss to depressed foragers, their jaws aching from chewing tough grains. They decide that the best thing now is to divide up the rice and mark off what shall belong to each.

This they do, but the failing which was the cause of all their woes as Radiant Beings reasserts itself anew. The word used to describe the Radiant Being who first tasted the protoplasmic earth – lolajātika – is now used to describe one who is not satisfied with the portion allotted to him. This person,

> *while looking after his own share, appropriated another which had not been given to him, and had the benefit of it. The others arraigned him and accused him of wrongdoing and told him not to do it again. He promised to reform but on being set free he transgressed a second and a third time. Again they took and chid him; but some used violence now, with hands and clods and sticks. Thus theft came into the world, and with it came censure and deceit and punishment.*

Brought to a new pitch of distress by this latest state of affairs, they meet once more, and this time they decide to confer authority on one from among themselves, empowering him to be the spokesman of their displeasure, and to deliver censure and to ordain banishment when these are justly deserved (there is no mention of any form of physical punishment). To compensate these responsibilities they will give over to him a portion of their shares of rice. The person to whom they go with their proposal is described as the handsomest, the most amiable, and the most capable of them all. The first title of this ruler is Mahā-sammata, meaning 'the great one appointed by the people'. His second title is Khattiya, meaning 'lord of the fields', *khettānam pati*. His third title is Rājā, from a word meaning delight – that is, delight in the Dhamma, than which, the Buddha declares, there is nothing higher, here or hereafter. This is said to be the origin of the highest caste.

Next the origins of the priestly caste are given. Disillusioned with life in society, a number of people decided to distance themselves from it. They went into the jungle and built shelters of leaves and devoted themselves to the contemplative life. This won them the admiration and respect of the populace. But not all of them were capable of meeting the demands of this way of life. Some returned from the jungle and set up on the outskirts of towns and villages, where they occupied themselves with the composition and repetition of texts. Thus the Vedas and the whole brahmanic system came about.

The two remaining castes are briefly dealt with. These are the farmers and merchants (*vessas*) and those who lead low lives in hunting and other bloody trades (*suddas*). Thus the classic four-caste system is derived from the myth of origins.

Then the story continues, and the formation of a fifth group, drawn from the others and unifying them all, is described. In the course of time a warrior came to be dissatisfied with his life-style and went forth from home into homelessness saying 'I will be a recluse.' Similarly a brahman, a vessa, and a sudda went forth. Thus from the four social groups, the circle of recluses, the *samaṇamaṇḍala*, came into being. Its rationale is that, contrary to general belief, caste-determined living in itself gives no assurance of salvation. Whatever their social origin, says the Buddha, the wicked will meet just retribution after death, while the good will go to heaven, if they have not attained to nibbāna in this life. Although this attainment is explicitly said to be possible for everyone, it is not on the basis of performing caste-duties but through being controlled in body, speech, and mind, for which membership of the samaṇamaṇḍala provides the most suitable milieu. This leads on to mention of the Buddhist monk (*bhikkhu*), the arahant living by right wisdom. Thus social development is said to culminate in this caste-free, selfless being and his group, the Buddhist Sangha, which takes the place of the circle of samaṇas as the caste-transcending community drawn from the whole of society.

Finally, we have the statement that the khattiyas are supreme – among the castes, that is, not absolutely:

Khattiyas are best of those who put trust in lineage;
the truly wise and good are best among gods and men.

The term 'khattiya' is usually translated as 'warrior'; but in the *Aggañña Sutta* this is not entirely satisfactory. It is said to have been derived from the expression 'khettānaṁ pati', Lord of the Fields, the significance of which is protective rather than combative. However, the word 'pati' has a depth of meaning which 'lord' in its modern sense has lost. Khettānaṁ pati comprises the meaning of 'husband of the fields', and so the title may have overtones of a sacred marriage between the ruler and the land, a notion not, of course, confined to ancient India. This deepens and enriches the idea of protectiveness. In the Sutta Piṭaka the relations commended to husbands with respect to their wives are not possessive but loving. If such relations have a bearing on those subsisting between the lord and the land, then we have to think of the khattiya's protectiveness as arising from love and not dominance, possessiveness, or acquisitiveness. If the term 'khattiya' is to be translated as 'warrior', its origin, as understood by the early Buddhists, must be clearly borne in mind: the khattiya is a protector first and always.

This, I believe, is the justification of the preference for the khattiyas over the brahmans: the view that the protecting rather than the sacrificing caste, or for that matter the trading or the labouring caste, bore the greatest burden of practical responsibility for the welfare of the world. The circle of the recluses, with liberated arahants at the centre, had responsibilities of another order, responsibilities the discharging of which made them the highest among gods and men; but in the practical sphere it was the warding warrior, sprung from the Lord of the Fields, from the husband of the land and the consort of the earth, who was called upon to administer the rule of righteousness.

Along with the idea of the protecting warrior in the *Aggañña Sutta* goes that of the king or rājā. But for the development of the idea of kingship we must turn to other discourses, those dealing with a figure of great appeal to the early Buddhists, the figure of the Universal Monarch, the Cakkavattin.

Here we have to bear in mind that the Buddha might, in the belief of his followers, have himself been a Cakkavattin if he had not chosen a higher way. What sort of rule he might have given the world was a question that occupied the minds of the more speculative among them.

Immediately preceding the *Aggañña Sutta* in the Canon is a discourse about a Universal Monarch (DN.xxvi). Although the story is an elaborate fable it contains some material relevant to this query. The king, named Dalhanemi, is ruler of the four quarters and protector of his people, whose conquests have been achieved not by the sword but by righteousness. Towards the end of a long life, Dalhanemi abdicates in favour of his eldest son and shaves his head and dons the yellow robes of a recluse and goes forth from home into homelessness. The son asks him what are the duties of a king. Dalhanemi exhorts him to live by the Dhamma, that is, righteously, which means being the protector of his people whatever their social status, with particular mention of the poor, who were to be assisted by the state. In addition, he is to be the protector of beasts and birds. This, it seemed to the early Buddhists, would have been the way of their leader. The new king fails to follow his father's advice, with dire consequences, as poverty gives rise to theft, violence, destructiveness, and all sorts of immorality.

The Buddha came of the khattiya caste. The universal ruler was called 'the Anointed Khattiya'. It was a very natural thing that the early community should assimilate each to the other. In this process there is to be discerned an ideal. It was an ideal which failed to find literary expression commensurate with its grandeur, but for a time it was to become a living reality in the person and in the policies of the Emperor Asoka, some two hundred years after the death of the Buddha.

Asoka was the grandson of Candragupta Maurya, who established an empire reaching from the Persian border eastward to the Ganges delta. Candragupta's career began with a war against the forces left by Alexander the Great in northern India. Then he turned south-east and conquered Magadha, where the Buddha had spent much of his life. When Asoka came to the throne he set out to extend the vast domain he had inherited. He went to war against Kalinga, to the south of his territories, where Orissa is today. By conventional standards the war was successful and Kalinga was added to the Mauryan empire. But the cost in blood and suffering was high and Asoka was touched with a sense of his own responsibility for it. He turned from the brahmanical view of kingship in which he had been trained, a view which made it the king's duty to fight aggressive wars and to acquire new territories. He adopted a view by which he became the protector of his people and by degrees the protector of other living beings in his dominions. Over and over again the message of non-violence, non-destructiveness, is repeated in the famous edicts which he had inscribed on rock and pillar throughout the empire. As it is good to be decent to servants, obedient to parents, generous to layfolk and religious, so it is good to refrain from killing living beings. Indeed the Seventh Pillar Edict states that abstention from injuring and slaying living beings is the characteristic way in which devotion to the Dhamma is demonstrated by Asoka's subjects. It has in fact been noted that abstention from killing is the article which occurs most frequently in the edicts. This promulgation of the First Sīla was not merely for public consumption. The emperor brought it home to his own court. As the First Rock Edict proclaims,

*No creature is to be slaughtered here in the capital city, Pataliputta
(the modern Patna).... Vast numbers of creatures used to be killed for
food every day in the royal kitchens. At present the number has been
reduced to three, two peacocks and a deer, and deer are not killed
regularly. In future none of these creatures is to be slaughtered.*

The Fifth Pillar Edict tells that twenty-six years after coming to power,
Asoka forbade the killing of certain creatures, including parrots and
minas, wild geese, bats, queen ants, terrapins, tortoises, porcupines,
squirrels, household animals, and all four-footed animals that are of no
use to man. Neither are nursing animals or their young to be killed.
Forests are not to be burned in order to kill their wild inhabitants;
neither are husks to be burned containing living creatures.

Living animals are not to be fed to other animals. On certain full-
moon days and other days, animals living in the elephant forests and
in the fishing preserves are not to be killed, nor, in the same days, are
fish. There were days also on which castration and branding were
forbidden.

From the Eighth Rock Edict we learn that on tours of his territories
the king did not, as his predecessors, pass the time in hunting and other
profane pleasures; instead he visited brahmans and samaṇas with gifts,
gave money to the elderly, and instructed country folk in the Dhamma.

Such was Asoka, the 'Beloved of the Gods', a unique figure in the
annals of Empire, and one which has haunted the Buddhist imagination ever since. With him the ideal of the khattiya comes perhaps as
close to realization as is possible in a world dominated by self-interest,
ill-will, and delusion. He is the man of power who turns from conquest
to protection, the contravener of the First Sīla who becomes its devoted
upholder.

This is a great story, and Asoka has been called the greatest of kings.
With his career in mind, the eulogy of the khattiyas in the *Aggañña Sutta*
would seem to be fully justified. However, this eulogy is not the high
point of the discourse. That in fact is the foundation of the
samaṇamaṇḍala, which looks forward to the Buddhist Sangha. The
samaṇamaṇḍala, 'truly wise and good', drawn from all four castes,
and including people who practised bloody trades but have abandoned them, is the social group that enables the others to transcend

* See Nikam and McKeon, *The Edicts of Asoka*, p.55.

their limitations and to encounter each other as equals. Society is thus conceived as a dynamic interactive organization which, however class-riven it may become, will always have one institution in which people of good will can meet each other away from the distorting influences of their particular groups. This institution in its historic form, the Sangha, may have other contributions to make to the welfare of society and beyond it to the world at large. This question will be examined in the next chapter.

7

A MEANINGFUL MYTH?

IN THE *Anguttara-Nikāya* there is an extended simile on the purification of the heart, comparing the process to the refining of gold, with the gradual removal of coarse and ever less coarse impurities until the gold dust alone remains, which is then melted in the crucible and poured out, giving a beautiful pliable substance capable of perfect workmanship. This is a vivid affirmation that the ground of human nature was seen as fundamentally good. But if there is gold in the ground there are also the roots of greed, hatred, and delusion, and it is on these that the *Aggañña Sutta* concentrates; necessarily so, its motive being a criticism of brahmanic pretensions and intolerance. But, as we have seen, the discourse goes far beyond this. Not only does it give a cosmology intelligible in terms of the ideas current at the time in India, but along with it, in effect, an anthropology too, using the word in something like its basic sense: an exposition of human nature. In seeking to find out in what ways the myth may be meaningful this would seem to be as good a starting point as any.

The Buddha's very high estimate of human worth gives positive force to his very unflattering view of human behaviour. The criticism is radical and challenging but based on the premise that right views and right effort can change behaviour and lead to freedom from errors that distort our lives and damage the lives and the world about us. If we do not deal with them we cannot even begin to be free. Wishing and even working to change the world is not enough.

Self-interest, ill-will, and self-deception pervade the activities of the beings in the *Aggañña Sutta* alike in their pre-human, their pre-sexual, and their fully human forms. They consume something they do not need or later they covet what is not theirs; they look down on others or later they drive them violently away; they repeat their mistakes over and over and fail to see this folly for what it is. Part of their folly is that they would rather feel sorry for themselves than accept responsibility for their actions and learn to see the connection between action and result. Their power of self-delusion seems to be virtually limitless. Perhaps the most disturbing aspect of the portrayal is this repetitiveness and this inability to see the pattern. These might be considered as a sort of behavioural echo of the cyclical repetitiveness of Indian cosmology, but they are also an illustration of an unhappy trend in human psychology, one that manifests itself all the time in personal, international, and environmental relations.

So the first way in which the myth may be described as meaningful is in showing us our own nature in an unfamiliar and provocative light. We ourselves are those beings who are driven by appetite, conceit, and stupidity; who make a mess of things time and again; who have a greater urge to lament than to reform.

But there is improvement too, and it shows in the language used of the first ruler chosen. Throughout the preceding part of the narrative the word by which the proud beings judge the others is based on the word for caste, *vaṇṇa*, which primarily signifies light or dark skin-colour. The pride of the light-coloured beings is called *vaṇṇatimāna*, a word which might be rendered as colour-consciousness, and it is specifically given as the cause of their troubles. But when later their successors come to choose a ruler this plays no part in their choice. True to type, they apply a criterion with a definite aesthetic element, but not one involving colour. We are told that the first ruler was well-formed, handsome, amiable, and capable, but not whether he was light or dark. This suggests an improvement in the moral make-up of the people since, with the development of sexuality, they became fully human; and it is meaningful in that it indicates a movement from a defective aesthetic standard of judgement to a more complete, partly ethical one.

The *Aggañña Sutta* differs from most myths in dealing with groups of beings and people and not with named individuals. The only one who stands out is the Chosen Ruler, and he has only titles indicating his status and epithets describing his qualities. This is not a disadvantage in considering a figure who is the prototype of the Good Ruler. An individualizing name might detract from this function. It is the titles and adjectives that matter.

The People's Choice, Guardian of the Fields, Delight in Justice: the titles speak for themselves. What of the epithets? Each of them means something, to be sure, but are they in any other sense meaningful? That depends on the scope we are prepared to allow them.

The first epithet (*abhirūpatara*) may be rendered as 'most vigorous in body'; the second (*dassanīyatara*) as 'best to look upon'; the third (*pāsādikatara*) as 'most pleasing to deal with'; the fourth (*mahesakkhatara*) as 'having the greatest authority'. Suitably reinterpreted they would describe good government at any time, and any society in which they were reflected would be a very fortunate one, for the ideas expressed in them are well-being, beauty, harmony, and capability. They produce an image of a society whose members enjoy the benefits of health, shelter, and security; which cherishes what is good in its heritage and adds to it for coming generations: which has a non-conflictual socio-economic ethos and a non-exploitative environmental one; which has just laws, an efficient civil service, and a government which respects the freedom of the individual citizen and the interests of neighbouring countries. Whether such a society has ever existed, even under the great Asoka, is a question I am not qualified to answer, but the *Aggañña Sutta* provides four words which at least enable us to conceive of it in imagination.

It may seem excessive to place such a burden on four adjectives, even if they are all superlatives. But the interpretation given above does contain a major Buddhist idea. Every system has key terms. On the religious side, if it has one, it may be faith, submission, election, ritual. On the social side it may be tribalism, individualism, communality, conformity. I believe that the Buddhist counterpart of these might be said to be mutuality, indicated above under the idea of harmony. Probably its most elaborate expression is found not in the Pāli Canon but in the voluminous *Avataṁsaka Sūtra** of the Mahāyāna with its image of Indra's Net, in which everything is reflected in everything

---

* Called the *Hwa Yen Sūtra* in China, where it gave rise to a sect also found in Japan, under the name Kegon. Garma C.C. Chang's *The Buddhist Teaching of Totality* provides an introduction to its ideas and a selection of its texts. The sūtra is usually referred to in English as the 'Garland Sūtra'.

else. Mutuality or interdependence is a recurrent theme in the *Aggañña Sutta* and the idea may be the most meaningful the discourse offers.

When the troubled first property-holders in the world choose a Protector they do not simply offer him a residence and an estate and a body of men as his agents and tell him to get on with it. What happens is that each one gives him a portion of his rice in return for the promise and practice of righteous rule. He puts his person, his qualities, and his power at their service and they supply him and, by implication, his family with sustenance. The relationship of the Protector and people is one of interdependence.

This relationship is seen again when the origin of the brahman caste is given. Although they retire from society and live in leaf-huts in the forest, the brahmans come into the settlements for food. They do not appear to contribute any visible benefit to society, their time being taken up with meditation, yet they are able to rely on society to support them. Clearly their withdrawal is not resented and their way of life commands respect. In Buddhist terms they offer an opportunity for giving, which is generally seen as a good thing in itself.

Even with the 'failed' brahmans the principle of interdependence holds, though here not without a suggestion of parasitism and exploitation. The people support them, but all they get in return is the chanting of texts made up by the brahmans and passed off as inspired.

As this becomes the norm in the course of time, it is no wonder that some members of the caste long for something better. For reasons not spelt out, people leave the other castes too and form a fifth group which is not called a caste but a circle, a maṇḍala. It seems to be a group with both an equalizing and a unifying function. This is its contribution to society, and what it gets, apart from sustenance, is nothing other than the members who make it up. It represents an advance on the old four-caste system and a corrective of its failings. It is at the same time an affirmation of the essential unity of the people, whatever their differences, and an outlet for those who wish to lead lives not determined by the duties and prejudices of caste.

The Buddhist Sangha is the samaṇamaṇḍala brought out of myth into history. But the member of the Sangha has a different title from samaṇa, recluse, though this continues to be used, most notably of the Buddha himself, who is often addressed as the Samaṇa Gotama. The new title is bhikkhu, from a word whose primary meaning is 'to share', but more than that, for it derives from a root which means 'to love' (*bhaj*) and thus its full meaning is 'to share lovingly'. The bhikkhu presents himself to members of all classes of society for alms, irrespective of what their diet and thus their offering may be, for all must be enabled to acquire merit by giving and, if they wish, to hear the Dhamma preached. What is given and received on each side is given and received with love. That is the feeling-tone of mutuality.

It seems to me that we have here the most fruitful message of the myth. The relations between the Sangha and the rest of society may offer a model of what mankind's relations with the world should be. In the interest of developing this model let us examine what the Canon tells us about the duties of the ordinary man as the early Buddhists conceived of them.

These duties are most comprehensively set out in the *Sigālovāda Sutta* (DN.xxxi), dealt with in some detail in an earlier chapter. This is one of the best-known texts in the Theravadin societies of South-east Asia and Sri Lanka and one which repays attention in any society.

We read that the Buddha was staying near Rajagaha, south of the Ganges, when on the way to the town he saw a young man named Sigāla worshipping with joined hands the six directions, east, south, west, north, nadir, and zenith, as he was enjoined by his late father to do. The Buddha is sympathetic, but suggests that Sigāla would honour his father's memory better if he did something more than just joining his hands and bowing or prostrating himself in the six directions. He takes a piece of ritual and transforms it into a rule of life, one that is imbued with the spirit of compassionate mutuality. It begins with the duties of children to parents, who represent the east where the sun, giver of light and sustainer of life, rises: I will support them as they supported me, keeping the family tradition worthily and making offerings in their name when they die. Correspondingly parents show their love by restraining their children from evil and encouraging them to be good, seeing to their education, arranging suitable marriages, and handing over their inheritance at the right time. The south represents the period of education, and the pupil shows regard for his teachers through politeness, eagerness to learn, and attention during lessons. Correspondingly, the teacher performs his duties conscientiously not only in teaching his pupils but in seeing to their safety, and he also praises their virtues to others. The west represents marriage, and the good husband is said to show respect for his wife by being courteous and faithful to her, by giving her authority, and by providing her with ornaments. She in turn performs her duties with skill and diligence, is hospitable to relations and neighbours, is faithful, and looks after his property. The north represents friendship, and there a person acts with generosity, courtesy, service, impartiality, and sincerity towards his friends and associates. They in turn look after him and his property when he behaves heedlessly, they provide refuge when he is in danger, they stand by him in times of trouble and see to his family's welfare. The nadir indicates the duties of masters and servants. The master assigns them work suitable to their abilities, provides food, pay, medical care, rest periods, and holidays, and shares with them any good fortune that comes his way. The workers for their part are prompt, industrious, and conscientious, they take only what is given them, and they do nothing to injure his good name. Finally, the zenith indicates the relations between a householder and holy men. His thoughts, words, and deeds in respect of them are kindly, he keeps open house for them and supplies their needs. The holy men for their part, like his parents before, restrain him from evil and encourage him to do good; they show their love for him by teaching him what he has not heard, by clarifying what he has heard, and by showing him the way to heaven.

The *Sigālovāda Sutta* amplifies the idea of mutuality found in the *Aggañña Sutta* and demonstrates in attractive detail its prevalence in the Buddhist world-view. While it deals explicitly with inter-human relations, its implications are far more extensive, not only socially but in other spheres of human activity. My concern here is with its implications for the natural world. Recalling the six directions, I think this concern is best elaborated in terms of the nadir and the zenith.

The nadir is predominantly the sphere of power. In the ideal scenario of the *Sigālovāda Sutta* we have employers and employees who are well-disposed to each other. But it covers all employment relations and by extension all relations in which one party is more powerful than the other. This is increasingly the relationship between man and the environment. As a result of technological empowerment, it has come more than ever to resemble the relationship between master and slave, with one party enjoying all the rights and making all the demands on the other. This in Buddhist terms cannot be good for either party, however much the master may approve or apparently benefit from it. There may be interdependence but it hardly deserves the name of mutuality. In every age, including the present, slaves have been abused, often worked, sometimes beaten, to death, and straightaway replaced by other slaves. The individuality of those men and women counted for nothing. The idea of slave-rights was simply beyond the range of human thought. It was one idea for which the Greeks did not have a word. To them – not only the Spartans with their periodic murders of the helots, but Socrates, Plato, Aristotle – the slave was a 'featherless biped' somewhere between real man and the ape. An analogy, not too far-fetched, can be seen in the way we have dealt with the world in respect of animal species, forests, and, increasingly, rivers and seas: when we have exterminated or destroyed or polluted one, we simply move on to another. The idea – the sense – of mutuality has been conspicuous by its absence in most of our dealings with the non-human world throughout most of history. It may have been stronger in primitive man than in his more technologically and religiously advanced successors. When a hunter brought down an animal with bow or spear and thanked it for giving itself as food for him and his people, he was expressing a relationship with nature not acknowledged in scientific theory or in the traditional grace before meat. He gave thanks directly to what sustained life directly. He may never have heard of the First Principle of Buddhism; he may indeed have been unable to conceive of a life without killing; but in his gratitude he was close to the great idea of mutuality, making a descent of sympathy to the non-human world such as the slave-owner typically could not make at the nadir in human relations.

Then what of the zenith? There is no specific mention of the Buddhist bhikkhu or Sangha in the *Sigālovāda Sutta*, only the general description 'ascetics and holy men'. This is the voice of the Indian tradition at its inclusive best and it goes without saying that the bhikkhu is counted among those who benefit from the layman's generosity and who benefit him in turn with counsel and instruction. We know from the Vinaya how a bhikkhu was to comport himself with lay people: for instance, the rules of etiquette when eating; the abstentions, as from attending public shows; the offences, such as the enticement of women or acting as a go-between; the injunctions against accepting too much food for his one daily meal or too many robes. What with all this and more, it seems that one function of the Discipline was to prevent the bhikkhu from becoming a burden and a nuisance to society. For a handful of food daily from a few people of all castes, and occasionally a length of cloth, he gives both opportunity to gain merit and the example of a frugal, modest life; he teaches the Dhamma to those who wish to hear it; he educates the young; he listens to people's troubles and helps settle their disputes; he comforts the dying and performs the funeral rites of the dead. The good bhikkhu gives so much in return for what he receives that it would not be easy to find a better model for mankind's relations with the rest of the world. But there is more to it than this. The bhikkhu is bound by the First Principle of his faith, that of non-injuriousness, so strictly that the first offence for which a novice may be expelled from the Order is the taking of the life of sentient beings. This ranks as more serious than theft, unchastity, and lies; than speaking ill of the Buddha, the Dhamma, and the Sangha. It is also an offence for the bhikkhu to destroy or damage plants or to foul drinking water.

These rules of the Discipline give substance to the suggestion that the relations of the Sangha with the community provides a model for man's relations with the natural world. The Sangha is part of society yet it preserves what might be called an internal distance from it. Man is part of the natural world but distinct from it by virtue of consciousness, purposiveness, and power, this last in many instances virtually abso-lute. The Buddhist layman finds himself between saddhamma and adhamma, the supreme law practised by the bhikkhus and the non-moral sphere of nature, the controlled way of life in which the smallest transgression must be accounted for and the domain of appetite where 'killing and devouring of the weak' is the necessary, blameless rule. He lives in tension between these two aspects of reality and has to take account of both. He derives sustenance from the animal and vegetal realms and from his surplus he helps support the Sangha. Directly or indirectly man and monk owe their lives to the natural world. The bhikkhu may not kill a living being or injure a growing plant. Not every layman is in a position to practise ahimsā to such a degree. But the ideal is there to be seen and pondered and as far as possible emulated. No matter what the layman does – it may be one of the 'bloody trades' such as hunting or slaughtering, or an otherwise destructive trade such as logging – there is this group of people who remind him that life can be lived without cruelty, destructiveness, and exploitation.

As the nadir is predominantly the sphere of power, so the zenith is pre-eminently the sphere of example. And it offers not only the exam-ple of conduct but that of reformation. In the *Aggañña Sutta* we have a criticism of brahmanism as the early Buddhists found it, that is, as a religion of power, its practitioners holding society in thrall with sacred texts and ritual, the latter based on sacrifice. But the Buddha was more than a critic. He was a reformer, and not only of institutions but of the world-view that inspired them. For the brahmanic urge to dominance he offered the ideas of co-operation and compassion. This brings reformation to the level of transformation, something more fundamental than changes in practice and opinion, nothing less than a revolution of consciousness with co-operation and compassion as its living principle.

8

CONCLUSION

THE BUDDHA MADE Right View the first element in the Noble Eightfold Path which leads to freedom. Thereby he gave primacy to knowledge in his system. In the *Mūlapariyāya Sutta* the nature of knowledge as conceived by the early Buddhists is set forth. The fields of knowledge named in the discourse are somewhat different from anything known to the modern world, or indeed to Western history, with the exception of the great elements, and earthly and spiritual beings. The essential difference lies not therein, however, but in the early Buddhists' view of knowledge. The modern world has come to accept that knowledge is power – power, that is, over the objective world, over external nature. To the early Buddhists such power was of no inherent value. Practical benefits might indeed accrue from it, but its pursuit was not to be undertaken by anyone aspiring to the highest life. The conquest of nature was not the way to freedom from sickness, old age, and death; rather it was a forging of chains for the spirit, a turning away from the possibility of freedom. Power over the roots of evil – greed, hatred, and delusion – was the only power they sought.

These three forces the Buddha saw working in all the relationships of man unfree, whether with his fellow beings or with the responsive earth or with himself. The Five Precepts were given to begin the process of reformation. The first precept calls for a new attitude to others – 'laying aside the cudgel to all living beings' is the recurrent phrase in which it is summed up. That this is in fact the first precept is a matter of incalculable importance. Nothing could demonstrate so potently the priority given by the Buddha to non-violence, non-hatred, non-destructiveness. From it, I believe, Buddhism derives a credibility that other religions lack when they discuss the relationship of man to the world about him. No reinterpretation of texts is required, no inflation of previously unconsidered phrases. The message has always been there, in the forefront, clear and uncompromising from the start. In respect of animals, it applies, as said before, whether or not the idea of a human–animal continuum is accepted.

The Buddha's teaching, which places so much emphasis on avoidance of extremes, is a counsel of balance and harmony. His life is conventionally described as a middle path between austerity and indulgence. It may also be understood in other ways, for a great life is a symbol with many aspects. I have endeavoured to present it as a harmonizing of civilization and nature, with delight as its keynote.

We in the West have never quite succeeded in achieving this. We have been dominated by two aggressive myths, one from the Hebrew and one from the Greek sources of our culture. The words of Genesis 1:28 leave no room for doubt as to the relationship deemed proper between man and his fellow beings:

> And God blessed them, and God said unto them, Be fruitful, and
> multiply, and replenish the earth, and subdue it; and have dominion
> over the fish of the sea, and over the fowl of the air, and over every
> living thing that moveth upon the earth.

Using the stolen Promethean fire, we have done this. But subjugation and domination are not self-limiting activities. There is no dividing line between them and destruction. In each there is the same absence of respect for anything beyond our own desires. From a Buddhist point of view, our dominant myths are both inadequate and pernicious.

The best that the Biblical myth has to offer, according to the new interpretation, is the idea of stewardship: henceforth man shall regard the earth and its creatures not merely as commodities to be wasted, consumed, and destroyed, but as gifts of God, who will one day ask him how well he took care of them. This is not a negligible idea. Certainly it is an advance on the teaching that 'God made the world to show his power and wisdom, and for man's use and benefit.' But it still suffers from the general failing of the Western conservationist ethos, which is based on human self-interest and not on respect for other life-forms for their own sake.

In contrast Buddhism offers the idea of the protector and the principle of mutuality. They arise naturally out of the *Aggañña Sutta* and are amplified in other discourses. Mutuality is an abiding element of the Dhamma. By contrast the figure of the khattiya is found only occasionally. But it is a noble idea, and indeed one which many people already live by and some have given their lives for. It is not, however, without its own peculiar dangers, for if the reproach of stewardship is self-interest, that of the protector of nature could be spiritual pride. Ideals attract not only those who aspire to them but also those who would soar beyond them into regions whose atmosphere can seem to be a rarefied and heady egoism. It may be salutary at times to remember that in the Buddhist myth the decline of the world is the result of pride and that the heart of the Buddha's message is compassion, not only for suffering nature but for erring men and women.

Compassion is the sentiment not only of mutuality but of the Middle Way in all its aspects. It spreads to all sides, even out to the extremes. These of course are to be avoided, but not the people found at the extremes. They are not to be shunned or vilified. That would only be another exercise of ill-will. The Buddha rubbed shoulders with some very extreme characters in the course of his eighty years. There was Ajātasattu the parricidal king; Angulimāla, a serial killer in a really big way; Devadatta the fanatic who tried to take over the Order and was prepared to kill the Buddha to do so. There no doubt were, and are, people who would have found the Buddha's friendship with Ambapālī the courtesan unbecoming in a moral guide. But the Buddha was neither a puritan nor a judge. He presents himself as the rediscoverer of an ancient law. The Dhamma teaches that those who do wrong shall requite it, either here or hereafter. The greater the wrong, the greater will be the requital, and so the greater should be the compassion.

This brings us finally to the question of time and duration in the Buddhist view of things.

However long or painful the requital of wrong may be, it will have an end. Good and evil are done in the domain of time and are requited in time. The Buddhist hells are as grim as anything in Dante but the doom of everlastingness does not lie over them. The idea of impermanence applies to them as to all other conditioned states. As the good come to the end of their merit, so the bad come to the end of their demerit. The wrongdoer always gets another chance. Even Devadatta will be saved. Only nibbāna, beyond good and evil, is said to transcend time, and in Buddhism time has a peculiar value, especially in its most enigmatic aspect – the present. Other religious systems proclaim that God – their particular God – created the world at some unspecified time in the past and will destroy it at some unspecified time in the future. Past and future each contain such an awesome moment that the present is inevitably overshadowed. The world exists because of God and will end because of God. Its existence is not only maintained but justified by God. It is not to be loved for its own sake; that would be idolatry. In Buddhism the case is different. The world exists because it exists. It exists in its own right and is to be accepted for its own sake. Its destiny is tragically involved with that of man as being not only the setting but even more the victim of his activities. It can do nothing of itself to change this relationship. That lies entirely with mankind. A fateful responsibility is thereby placed upon us, one whose demands we shall always find hard to meet given the roots of greed, hatred, and delusion in our hearts. But the message of the Dhamma is that these roots can be removed, that the ground of our nature is good and rich in gold. The qualities needed to meet the responsibility can be developed; the material is there. And the most important time is not in the past or future but in the present, every moment containing the beginning and end of things. More than most religions Buddhism has always had a sense of the true vastness of time. Where other religions talk in terms of generations and millennia, it comprehends astronomical periods and shapes its thinking accordingly. But it also gives a unique importance to the passing moment, the atoms and sub-atoms of time that make up those aeons. The slightest acquaintance with Buddhist meditation will leave no doubt as to the importance set on the present. Each passing moment is quite literally a challenge to the meditator. However trivial its content, however flat its feeling, it is to receive all the attention one can give it, because it is there. This is all of a piece with the Buddhist attitude to the world. Was it created out of nothing? Will it end in fire from heaven? These are of no importance beside the fact that it is. Its existence is its justification. Its value lies not in its origin or its end but in its present. Gods may stand at each extreme, but the present is the domain of man and the fate of the world is decided in every moment.

AFTERWORD

SOME OF THE BUDDHA'S early followers believed that the Teaching would flourish for only 500 years, after which it would go into a long decline. This apprehension proved prophetically true in India itself. What they failed to foresee, however, was that the Teaching would spread to other parts of Asia and many centuries later to the unknown continents of Europe and America. As it spread the Teaching would change and develop to meet the needs of widely different peoples while retaining the essentials of the Buddha's vision. The attraction of an individual today to one or another school of Buddhism is probably as much a matter of temperament as of doctrine. The Theravāda of South-east Asia, the Mahāyāna of Japan, and the Vajrayāna of Tibet have each their particular atmosphere with its particular appeal.

Like all the great religions in the materialistic modern world, Buddhism has been in better state than now we find it. It has had to endure many trials down the centuries, from misrepresentation to persecution on a massive scale, in ancient and modern times. Still it lives on, and here and there it even thrives. There is something in this old Teaching that commends itself to individuals in every generation. Even if Buddhism had died out, as the most pessimistic of the early followers expected, the voice of the Buddha would still be heard, for it is not confined within dedicated institutions and professing populations. It is a universal voice, and its message is greater than anything that might claim to contain it in its entirety. Wherever compassion, generosity, open-mindedness, and freedom are living values the message is honoured. Where they are rejected it is persecuted.

It is said that when Christian missionaries first went to Buddhist lands they were not only welcomed as honoured guests but were helped by local people to build their churches and living quarters. This was thought to be a sign that the people were eager for a higher truth and would soon be converted. It was in fact the expression of a generosity of spirit infused by the Buddha into his message, something the missionaries found hard to understand. In fact they found the whole culture of Buddhism different from anything they had known: goodness without the threat of hell, justice without the intervention of prophets, salvation without the help of God. Such was the general thinking of the time in Christianity – as it still is in some sects – that this way of life and the religion informing it were deemed to be evil and their destruction to be good. Buddhism was compared to the upas tree, which is said to poison everything in its shade.

Misunderstanding and hostility at this level are bad enough. But Buddhism was not always fortunate in its friends either. Early in the nineteenth century Arthur Schopenhauer wrote one of the most influential of all philosophical works, *Die Welt als Wille und Vorstellung* ('The World as Will and Representation'). In it, though only imperfectly acquainted with the religion – inevitably so, given the state of knowledge at the time – he more or less assimilated Buddhism to his pessimistic view of life. If he played the greatest part in making the Teaching intellectually respectable in Europe, it was at a price. Schopenhauer's influence extended beyond philosophy into the arts, and some of the greatest names in music and literature over the past 150 years have owed a debt to him. Whether Buddhism does must be debatable. Reading Schopenhauer one can feel as if he confined himself to the first of the Noble Truths, that of dukkha. He believed nirvāṇa to be another word for nothingness. One can feel that his attraction for Buddhism was as much temperamental as intellectual and that his understanding of it was largely shaped by the dubious light of a constitutional gloom.*

---

* See Thomas Mann's introduction to *The Living Thoughts of Schopenhauer*. The philosopher thought the Buddhists (and the Hindus with their 'reabsorption in Brahma') to be evasive in their terminology and unwilling to call nothingness by its real name (ibid. p.114). One wonders if he knew about the jhānas and the 'nothingness' (ākiñcañña) which characterizes one of them, but not the final one, much less nibbāna.

Another German writer, George Grimm, who came to Buddhism via Schopenhauer, is illuminating on the relationship between the philosopher and the Dhamma, in his *The Doctrine of the Buddha*.

But an individual coming to Buddhism by way of Schopenhauer – not only a great philosopher but a most persuasive writer – would not be coming to anything like a living form of it. The atmosphere of Buddhism, where allowed to function naturally, is normally relaxed and happy, reflecting the temperament of the Founder, one of the standard epithets for whom is Sugata, meaning the Happy One.

As the nineteenth century wore on more of the literature became available in the West as a succession of great scholars applied themselves to its study and translation. Thanks to their work almost solely, the Teaching became better known and won more adherents. This coincided with the diffusion of vegetarian ideas on the one hand and of concern about the treatment of animals in the biological sciences on the other. As thinking people became more aware of this abuse they looked for an idea to set against the triumphant course of the experimentalists, and the only system that had such an idea at its heart was Buddhism. Compassion and non-injuriousness, ahiṁsā, ruled the lives of these early Western believers.

The form of Buddhism best known at that time was the Theravāda, with its scriptures in Pāli. This was an indirect result of the fact that much of the Theravadin domain – Burma, Ceylon, Indo-China – was occupied by the British and French. Among the bureaucrats, soldiers, planters, and missionaries sent out by the colonial powers there were outstanding scholars and they did much of the pioneering work from which we are still benefiting.

Late in the nineteenth century the Buddhism of China and Japan, the Mahāyāna, became better known. Lafcadio Hearn, with his sympathetic insight and fine style, is among the most readable of writers on Buddhism. Then came D.T. Suzuki, whose books on Zen have had a remarkable popularity among three generations of seekers and whose ideas won the admiration of Martin Heidegger. If the Theravāda embodies pre-eminently the ethical aspect of Buddhism, the Mahāyāna developed its aesthetic potential to levels of refinement unsurpassed in the history of art.

With the fall of Tibet the Vajrayāna was brought to the West, a rich development of Buddhism, as different from the Theravāda as the Orthodox Church is from Methodism. But however much the outer forms may differ, at heart the message is the same: that every sentient being is to be treated with compassion and that the fact of common existence is more important than differences of species or classification.

All these traditions are now to be found outside their Asian home-lands. It may well be said that the Wheel of the Law has made its first full turn in the West. We now know much more of the fullness of Buddhism, its simplicities and riches, than was known when the beauty of ahiṁsā first drew troubled individuals to the Teaching. We know too that ahiṁsā is not as simple an idea as we might wish. It does not exist in the natural world where necessity rules and one species must live off another. It is an ethical principle conceived by human beings and therefore its application will always be imperfect. As the second turn-ing of the Wheel commences those to whom ahiṁsā is still the most important element in Buddhism will have to take into account factors that simply did not exist in the nineteenth century. Not only they but all other thinking Buddhists will have to face challenges not known before in human history. We have an idea what some of these will be because – in prototype, so to say – they are here already, and are making all systems, philosophical, social, and religious, look anew at their fundamental tenets to find meaningful responses. The greatest or at any rate the most conspicuous of these challenges lies in the field of genetics. Already the bounds between genera have been crossed with the implantation of human genes in animals. Some people will see this as validating at one level what Indian religion accepted at another: science catching up with mythology, as it were. Then there is the prospect, if not already the fact, of genetic alteration in human beings. What implications has this for the various models of human nature that philosophy and religion have given us? The theist may ask, What becomes of the personal soul if the potential person can be changed into someone else at the very beginning of life? The Buddhist may ask, What becomes of personal karma if, in effect, that shaping inheritance can be modified in the genes? These and other questions face mankind with a very troubled prospect in the coming years. It has a qualitative feel to it, different in kind from anything we have known hitherto. It may not be too much to say that the challenge to our inner resources is greater than at any time since the human mind fashioned its creation myths to make sense of a bewildering world. Imagination was the decisive factor when man first came to terms with his environment, a force that imposed vital order on raw chaos. Something similar may be required again. This time, however, imagination will not have to bear the burden unaided. We have the insights of the great religions and philosophies to help us. We shall need all this help, believer, unbeliever, and sceptic together. We cannot wish the future away. Mankind chose to take the flight of knowledge. The vehicle flies from one scientific advance to the next and ordinary mortals seem to have little or no say in its direction. When eventually it touches down – safely, let us hope as so many of the advances have a destructive aspect – we shall find a very perplexing moral and intellectual landscape. Dukkha in new and strange guises will make unprecedented demands on all mankind and all belief-systems. In the light of new discoveries, we can expect re-examinations of doctrine, painful adjustments with perhaps some uneasy apologetic, and all the other signs of religions in travail. Buddhism will have to go through the same ordeal as the other faiths. It has however two great supports to help it face the future.

One of the Signs of Being in the Doctrine is Impermanence. This does not only mean that all things pass away. It also means that as long as they last they are forever changing. Thus change is seen as an inherent condition in all forms, all institutions. It is accepted as the most natural thing in life; not something enforced from outside but arising from within. Accordingly it may be viewed in a positive way, as a factor in recreating individuals, institutions, even belief-systems to meet a changing world.

The second support is the word of the Buddha himself that his doctrine is timeless – akālika Dhamma. This, coming from the highest source, is the strongest possible reinforcement for what has just been said, even if it presents us with a paradox, the complementarity of impermanence and timelessness. The Dhamma, while endlessly adaptable, has a value for the world which the passing of time cannot remove, for its principles do not change, nor the order in which they stand. The First Principle will always be non-injuriousness: abstaining from violence and living with compassion for all sentient beings, however strangely in the future the lives of some of them may be brought about.

SELECT BIBLIOGRAPHY

Canonical texts are published by the Pali Text Society, London, unless otherwise stated.

PĀLI TEXTS

Dīgha-Nikāya, ed. T.W. Rhys Davids and J. Estlin Carpenter, 3 vols., 1971–3
Majjhima-Nikāya, ed. V. Trenckner, 3 vols., 1888–1899
Saṁyutta-Nikāya, ed. Leon Feer, 5 vols., 1884–1898
Aṅguttara-Nikāya, ed. Rev. Richard Morris and E. Hardy, 5 vols., 1888–1900
Sutta-Nipāta, ed. Dines Andersen and Helmer Smith, 1965

TRANSLATIONS USED OR CONSULTED
Digha-Nikāya:
   T.W. and C.A.F. Rhys Davids, *Dialogues of the Buddha*, 3 vols., 1971–3
   Steven Collins, 'The Discourse on What is Primary (Aggañña-Sutta)',
      Journal of Indian Philosophy, vol.21, no.4, December 1993
Majjhima-Nikāya:
   I.B. Horner, *The Collection of Middle Length Sayings*, 3 vols., 1957–1967
   Bhikkhu Sīlācāra, *The First Fifty Discourses*, Walter Markgraf, Breslau 1912
Saṁyutta-Nikāya:
   C.A.F. Rhys Davids and F.L. Woodward, *The Book of the Kindred Sayings*, 5
      vols., 1965–1975
Aṅguttara-Nikāya:
   F.L. Woodward and E.M. Hare, *The Book of the Gradual Sayings*, 5 vols.,
      1970–5
Khuddaka-Nikāya:
   S. Radhakrishnan, *Dhammapada*, Oxford University Press, London 1950
   Khuddakapāṭha: Ñānamoli, *Minor Readings*, London 1960
   Sutta-Nipāta: V. Fausböll, *A Collection of Discourses*, Clarendon, Oxford 1881
   Therī/Theragāthā: C.A.F. Rhys Davids, *Psalms of the Early Buddhists*, 1964

Udāna and Itivuttaka: F.L. Woodward, *Verses of Uplift* and *As It Was Said*,
  Geoffrey Cumberlege for Oxford University Press, London 1948
Vinaya:
  T.W. Rhys Davids and Hermann Oldenberg, *Vinaya Texts*, 3 vols.,
  Clarendon Press, Oxford, 1881–1885

OTHER WORKS

Appleyard, Brian, *Understanding the Present: Science and the Soul of Modern
  Man*, Picador, London 1992
Babbitt, Irving, *Representative Writings*, ed. George A. Panichas, University of
  Nebraska, Lincoln, Nebraska 1981
Bacon, Francis, *The Advancement of Learning*, ed. G.W. Kitchin, J.M. Dent,
  London 1915
Bapat P.V. et al., *2500 years of Buddhism*, Government of India, Delhi 1959
Barthes, Roland, *Mythologies*, Peter Smith, London 1983
Bouquet, A.C., *Comparative Religion*, Penguin, Harmondsworth 1962
Budiansky, Stephen, *The Covenant of the Wild: Why Animals Chose
  Domestication*, Weidenfeld and Nicolson, London 1992
Chang, Garma C.C., *The Buddhist Teaching of Totality: The Philosophy of Hwa
  Yen Buddhism*, Allen and Unwin, London 1972
Kenneth K.S. Ch'en, *Buddhism in China*, Princeton University Press,
  Princeton, New Jersey 1964
Conze, Edward, *Buddhism: Its Essence and Development*, Bruno Cassirer,
  Oxford 1974
Conze, Edward, *Buddhist Scriptures*, Penguin, Harmondsworth 1975
Conze, Edward, *A Short History of Buddhism*, Allen and Unwin, London 1980
Coomaraswamy, A.K. and Sister Nivedita, *Myths of the Hindus and Buddhists*,
  Dover Publications, New York 1967
Eliade, Mircea, *From Primitives to Zen*, Collins, London 1967
Feuerstein, Georg, *The Essence of Yoga*, Rider, London 1974
Grimm, George, *The Doctrine of the Buddha*, Akademie-Verlag, Berlin 1958
Guenther, Herbert V. *Buddhist Philosophy in Theory and Practice*, Penguin,
  Harmondsworth 1972
Hearn, Lafcadio, *The Buddhist Writings of Lafcadio Hearn*, Wildwood House,
  London 1981
Hopkins, E. Washburn, *Ethics of India*, Yale University Press, Newhaven 1924
Horner I.B., *Early Buddhism and the Taking of Life*, Buddhist Publication
  Society, Kandy, Sri Lanka 1967
Jayatilleke, K.N., *Early Buddhist Theory of Knowledge*, Allen and Unwin,
  London 1963
Johansson, Rune E.A., *The Psychology of Nirvana*, Allen and Unwin, London
  1969
Karunatilake, H.N.S., *The Confused Society*, Buddhist Information Centre, Sri
  Lanka 1976
Knights, L.C., *Explorations*, Chatto and Windus, London 1963

Küng, Hans, *Global Responsibility: In Search of a New World Ethic*, SCM Press, London 1991

Law, Bimala C., *Geography of Early Buddhism*, Kegan Paul, London 1932

Law, Bimala C., *Some Kśatriya Tribes of Ancient India*, Calcutta and Simla 1923

Law, Bimala C., *History of Pali Literature*, Kegan Paul, London 1933

Ling, Trevor, *The Buddha: Buddhist Civilization in India and Ceylon*, Penguin, Harmondsworth 1976

Malalasekera, G.P., *Aspects of Reality as Taught by Theravada Buddhism*, Buddhist Publication Society, Kandy, Sri Lanka 1968

Maurice, David (U Ohn Ghine), *The Lion's Roar: An Anthology of the Buddha's Teachings, selected from the Pali Canon*, Rider, London 1962

Murti, T.R.V., *The Central Philosophy of Buddhism*, Allen and Unwin, London 1974

Ñānamoli, Bhikkhu, *A Thinker's Note Book*, The Forest Hermitage, Kandy, Sri Lanka 1971

Northrop, F.S.C., *The Meeting of East and West*, Macmillan, New York 1946

Nikam, N.A. and McKeon, R. (eds.), *The Edicts of Asoka*, University of Chicago Press, 1959

Nyānaponika, Thera, *Abhidhamma Studies*, Freewin, Dodanduwa, Sri Lanka 1949

Nyānaponika Thera, *Satipatthana: The Heart of Buddhist Meditation*, 'The Word of the Buddha' Publishing Committee, Colombo 1953

Ortega y Gasset, Jose, *Meditations on Hunting*, Charles Scribner's Sons, New York 1972

Otto, Rudolph, *The Idea of the Holy*, Oxford University Press, 1950

Rhys Davids, C.A.F., *Indian Religion and Survival*, Allen and Unwin, London 1934

Robinson, Richard H., *The Buddhist Religion: A Historical Introduction*, Dickinson, Belmont, California 1970

Saddhatissa, Ven. H., *Buddhist Ethics*, Allen and Unwin, London 1970

Sangharakshita, *A Survey of Buddhism*, Windhorse, Glasgow 1993

Scheler, Max, *Man's Place in Nature*, trans. Hans Meyerhoff, Farrar Straus and Giroux, New York 1981

Schopenhauer, Arthur, *The Living Thoughts of Schopenhauer*, ed. Thomas Mann, Cassell, London 1946

Schumacher, E.F., *Small is Beautiful*, Abacus, London 1974

Schweitzer, Albert, *Civilization and Ethics*, A&C Black, London 1949

Sīlācāra, Bhikkhu, *The Noble Eightfold Path*, Theosophical Publishing House, Adyar, Madras, India 1915

Story, Francis, *Dimensions of Buddhist Thought*, Buddhist Publication Society, Kandy, Sri Lanka 1975

Sullivan, J.W.N., *The Limitations of Science*, Penguin, Harmondsworth 1938

Suzuki, D.T., *Outlines of Mahayana Buddhism*, Schocken, New York 1973

Thomas, P., *Epics, Myths and Legends of India*, D.P. Taraporevala and Sons, Bombay 1961

Thomas, Edward J., *The Life of Buddha as Legend and History*, Routledge and
   Kegan Paul, London 1975
Tucci, Giuseppe, *The Theory and Practice of the Mandala*, Rider, London 1961
Warder, A.K., *Indian Buddhism*, Motilal Banarsidass, Delhi 1970
Warren, Henry Clarke, *Buddhism in Translations*, Harvard University Press,
   Cambridge, Mass. 1922
Watts, Alan, *Nature, Man and Woman*, Wildwood House, London 1973
Wickramasinghe, Martin, *Aspects of Sinhalese Culture*, Tisara Prakasakayo
   Dehiwara, Sri Lanka 1973
Zaehner, R.C., *Mysticism Sacred and Profane*, Oxford University Press, London
   1961

INDEX

The Windhorse symbolizes the energy of the enlightened mind carrying the Three Jewels – the Buddha, the Dharma, and the Sangha – to all sentient beings.

Buddhism is one of the fastest growing spiritual traditions in the Western world. Throughout its 2,500-year history, it has always succeeded in adapting its mode of expression to suit whatever culture it has encountered.

Windhorse Publications aims to continue this tradition as Buddhism comes to the West. Today's Westerners are heirs to the entire Buddhist tradition, free to draw instruction and inspiration from all the many schools and branches. Windhorse publishes works by authors who not only understand the Buddhist tradition but are also familiar with Western culture and the Western mind.

For orders and catalogues contact

WINDHORSE PUBLICATIONS
11 PARK ROAD
BIRMINGHAM
B13   8AB
UK

WINDHORSE PUBLICATIONS INC
540 SOUTH 2ND WEST
MISSOULA
MT 59802
USA

Windhorse Publications is an arm of the Friends of the Western Buddhist Order, which has more than forty centres on four continents. Through these centres, members of the Western Buddhist Order offer regular programmes of events for the general public and for more experienced students. These include meditation classes, public talks, study on Buddhist themes and texts, and 'bodywork' classes such as t'ai chi, yoga, and massage. The FWBO also runs several retreat centres and the Karuna Trust, a fund-raising charity that supports social welfare projects in the slums and villages of India.

Many FWBO centres have residential spiritual communities and ethical businesses associated with them. Arts activities are encouraged too, as is the development of strong bonds of friendship between people who share the same ideals. In this way the FWBO is developing a unique approach to Buddhism, not simply as a set of techniques, less still as an exotic cultural interest, but as a creatively directed way of life for people living in the modern world.

If you would like more information about the FWBO please write to

LONDON BUDDHIST CENTRE
51 ROMAN ROAD
LONDON
E2 0HU
UK

ARYALOKA
HEARTWOOD CIRCLE
NEWMARKET
NH 03857
USA

ALSO FROM WINDHORSE

SANGHARAKSHITA

THE TEN PILLARS OF BUDDHISM

The Ten Pillars of Buddhism are ten ethical principles which together provide a comprehensive guide to the moral dimension of human life.

To explore them is to turn the lens of moral vision on to one aspect of life after another. To apply them is to accept the challenge of human potential for higher development – and to work with that challenge in the arena of everyday life.

Readers from the Buddhist world will find some of Sangharakshita's ideas especially thought-provoking – and even controversial. But all readers, whether Buddhists or not, will find this essay an invaluable source of stimulation and insight in their quest for ethical standards by which to live.

112 pages
ISBN 1 899579 21 4
£5.99/$11.95

KAMALASHILA

MEDITATION: THE BUDDHIST WAY OF TRANQUILLITY AND INSIGHT

A comprehensive guide to the methods and theory of Buddhist meditation, written in an informal, accessible style. It provides a complete introduction to the basic techniques, as well as detailed advice for more experienced meditators seeking to deepen their practice. The author is a long-standing member of the Western Buddhist Order, and has been teaching meditation since 1975. In 1979 he helped to establish a semi-monastic community in North Wales, which has now grown into a public retreat centre. For more than a decade he and his colleagues developed approaches to meditation that are firmly grounded in Buddhist tradition but readily accessible to people with a modern Western background. Their experience – as meditators, as students of the traditional texts, and as teachers – is distilled in this book.

304 pages, with charts and illustrations
ISBN 1 899579 05 2
£12.99/$25.95

SANGHARAKSHITA

TRANSFORMING SELF AND WORLD:

THEMES FROM THE SUTRA OF GOLDEN LIGHT

As the earth's resources are wasted and defiled, as the nations of the world are ravaged by war and hunger, we can afford to give way neither to cynicism nor to despair. The Utopian longings of the sixties may be a romantic memory, but we still need to change the world.

With skill and clarity, Sangharakshita translates the images and episodes of the beautiful but mysterious *Sutra of Golden Light* into a commentary filled with practical insights into many contemporary dilemmas, while losing none of the potent magic of the original sutra.

240 pages, illustrated
ISBN 0 904766 73 X
£10.99/$21.95

SANGHARAKSHITA

A SURVEY OF BUDDHISM:

ITS DOCTRINES AND METHODS THROUGH THE AGES

Now in its seventh edition, *A Survey of Buddhism* continues to provide an indispensable study of the entire field of Buddhist thought and practice. Covering all the major doctrines and traditions, both in relation to Buddhism as a whole and to the spiritual life of the individual Buddhist, Sangharakshita places their development in historical context. This is an objective but sympathetic appraisal of Buddhism's many forms that clearly demonstrates the underlying unity of all its schools.

'It would be difficult to find a single book in which the history and development of Buddhist thought has been described as vividly and clearly as in this survey.... For all those who wish to "know the heart, the essence of Buddhism as an integrated whole", there can be no better guide than this book.' *Lama Anagarika Govinda*

'I recommend Sangharakshita's book as the best survey of Buddhism.' *Dr Edward Conze*
544 pages
ISBN 0 904766 65 9
£12.99, $24.95

SANGHARAKSHITA

THE DRAMA OF COSMIC ENLIGHTENMENT:

PARABLES, MYTHS, AND SYMBOLS OF THE WHITE LOTUS SUTRA

The *White Lotus Sutra* tells the greatest of all stories, that of human life and human potential. Taking the entire cosmos for its stage and all sentient beings for its players, the Sutra illuminates a strange realm indeed, but its parables, myths, and symbols have made it loved and revered throughout the Buddhist world.

In this commentary, Sangharakshita brings these parables, myths, and symbols to vivid life and shows how they relate to our own spiritual quest. The discussions that follow each chapter draw us deeper into the true meaning of the Sutra, the precious significance of our lives.

As befits a tradition of devotion to the Sutra over the centuries, every page is beautifully decorated with lino-cut motifs.

240 pages, illustrated
ISBN 0 904766 59 4
£8.99/$15.99

ANDREW SKILTON (STHIRAMATI)

A CONCISE HISTORY OF BUDDHISM

How and when did the many schools and sub-sects of Buddhism emerge? How do the ardent devotion of the Pure Land schools, the magical ritual of the Tantra, or the paradoxical negations of the Perfection of Wisdom literature, relate to the direct, down to earth teachings of Gautama the 'historical' Buddha? Did Buddhism modify the cultures to which it was introduced, or did they modify Buddhism?

Here is a narrative that describes and correlates the diverse manifestations of Buddhism – in its homeland of India, and in its spread across Asia, from Mongolia to Sri Lanka, from Japan to the Middle East. Drawing on the latest historical and literary research, Andrew Skilton explains the basic concepts of Buddhism from all periods of its development, and places them in a historical framework.

272 pages, with maps and extensive bibliography
ISBN 0 904766 92 6
£9.99/$19.95